Country
New England
Antiques, Crafts
and
Factory Outlets

Country
New England
Antiques, Crafts
and
Factory Outlets

by

Anthony Hitchcock

and

Jean Lindgren

BURT FRANKLIN & CO.

© 1978 by Burt Franklin & Co., Inc.

235 East Forty-fourth Street
New York, New York 10017

Library of Congress Cataloging in Publication Data

Hitchcock, Anthony,
Country New England antiques, crafts, and
factory outlets.

(The Compleat traveler's companion)
1. Antiques—New England—Directories.
2. Handicraft—New England—Directories.
3. Shopping—New England—Directories.
I. Lindgren, Jean,   – joint author.
II. Title.   III. Series.
NK810.H57   380.1'45'74502574   78-6502
ISBN 0-89102-141-8
ISBN 0-89102-137-X pbk.

Designed by Bernard Schleifer

Printed in the United States of America

Contents

Introduction

SHOPPING IN New England is one of our favorite pastimes. Whether attending a local country auction, shopping in one of the many antiques and crafts shops, or finding a rock-bottom bargain at a factory store, this region provides a greater range of offerings in a relatively small area than any other we know of in the country.

Virtually gone, however, are the days when an antiques-lover could drive to the farther reaches of New England and wrest a valuable item from someone's attic for a song. The value of antiques is recognized by both sellers and buyers alike, and local sellers are getting the fair prices that their treasures have so long deserved.

New England has the large number of antiques dealers one would expect in an area that is visited by so many tourists each year. As you browse from shop to shop, we suggest you observe some basic rules for purchasing any antique of more than merely nominal value. If you plan to buy a piece for which you will spend a premium because it is particularly indicative of a style or period, do not buy on impulse. If the piece appears to be an unusual bargain, there is probably a reason. Ask the pertinent questions: Has it been repaired? Is it entirely original? Are these the original brasses or other hardware? Is this the original finish or paint? Are you buying from a reputable dealer—and will the bill of sale guarantee the authenticity of the antique? We feel that any reputable dealer will be more than happy to take back any item that is not as described. Because we are not professional dealers, we would not buy any but the least important piece without such an assurance in writing.

If you are new to antiques-collecting, you may enjoy two books that we have found particularly helpful: *The Insider's Guide to Antiques, Art and Collectibles,* by Sylvia O'Neill Dorn (Garden City, N.Y.: Doubleday, 1974), which offers a thorough discussion of how and from whom to buy antiques, and *The Impecunious Collector's Guide to American Antiques,* by John T. Kirk (New York: Alfred A. Knopf, 1975), a nicely illustrated guide for the new collector that gives, in a refreshing way, the philosophy of antiques: what makes an antique, how to buy antiques, and what to do (and not to do) after acquiring them.

American handicrafts are in their renaissance period. There are probably more handcrafted items available in this country now than at any other time since the Industrial Revolution. Throughout New England you will find thousands of craftspeople who are proud to have "escaped from the rat race" and are now making smaller but, perhaps, more satisfying incomes with their own hands. There is a tremendous range of quality in crafts that are offered in shops and studios. Here, however, the buyer may rely more safely on his or her personal taste and weigh the price directly against desire. Certainly this is true of functional crafts, which dominate the crafts market as a whole. When attending a crafts show, it is helpful to know if it is an "open" show or a "juried" show. The latter only accepts a fixed number of craftspeople, who must first submit either their actual works or a set of slides to be judged by an impartial jury of craftspeople. The overall quality of this type of show is likely to be higher, although the open shows are often just as much fun.

Factory stores are a phenomenon that is definitely on the increase. Many firms now realize the sales potential of offering their products, especially the irregulars, at discount prices right at the mill, thereby reducing handling costs. Other shops have opened up as "mill to you" outlets with almost as great savings. Both types of outlets are listed in this book. The single most important bit of advice we have for shopping in these stores is to look for and discover the irregularity. (If you are not certain if the product being offered is a first or a second, ask.) If it is a second, make sure you will be as happy to wear or use it as you are with the savings you are receiving.

The wide range of shops that follows only hints at the wealth of opportunities that await you in New England. Use these as starting points and then branch off on your own. Don't hesitate to ask one shop to recommend other reputable dealers. Generally speaking, friendships among dealers are stronger than competition.

For the convenience of readers, this volume has been organized as a companion to the others in this series. The material is arranged by states; within each state, by regions; and within a region, by towns and villages. If you have trouble finding a town, check the index, where all are listed alphabetically after the name of their state.

We have made every effort to provide information as carefully and accurately as possible, but we remind readers that all prices, items offered, and store hours are subject to change. Many dealers often attend antiques and crafts shows or auctions away from their hometown. Prospective visitors are urged to call in advance before traveling any great distance to a shop. In addition, particular offerings of shops are listed simply to give an indication to readers of the sort of selections typical of the shop, not as specific items for sale. Further, we have neither solicited nor accepted any fees or gratuities for inclusion in this or any of the other books in this series. Should readers wish to suggest corrections for future editions or offer their own comments, we welcome their correspondence. Please write to us in care of our publishers—Artemis Books, 235 East 44th Street, New York, N.Y. 10017.

We hope you enjoy your shopping as much as we have enjoyed visiting and talking with the shopkeepers throughout this region.

Anthony Hitchcock
Jean Lindgren

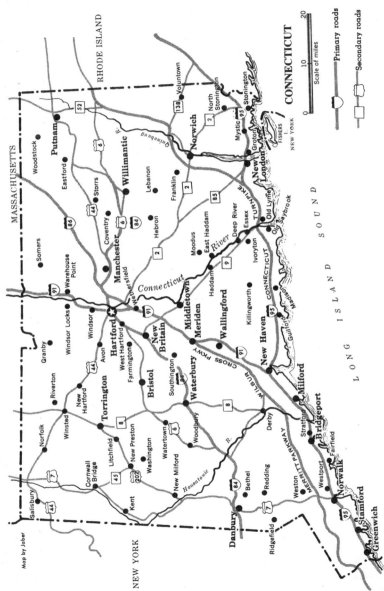

CONNECTICUT

Scale of miles

0   10   20

Primary roads

Secondary roads

MASSACHUSETTS

RHODE ISLAND

NEW YORK

LONG ISLAND SOUND

FISHERS I.
NEW YORK

Map by Jaber

Woodstock
Putnam
Eastford
Storrs
Willimantic
Lebanon
Franklin
Norwich
North Stonington
Stonington
Mystic
New London
Groton
Voluntown

Somers
Warehouse Point
Coventry
Manchester
Hebron
Moodus
East Haddam
Deep River
Essex
Old Lyme
Old Saybrook

Granby
Windsor Locks
Windsor
Hartford
Wethersfield
Middletown
Haddam
Ivoryton

Riverton
New Hartford
Avon
West Hartford
Farmington
New Britain
Meriden
Wallingford
Killingworth

Norfolk
Winsted
Torrington
Bristol
Southington
Waterbury
New Haven

Salisbury
Cornwall Bridge
Litchfield
New Preston
Washington
Watertown
Woodbury
Derby
Milford

Kent
New Milford
Stratford
Bridgeport
Fairfield

Ridgefield
Danbury
Bethel
Redding
Weston
Westport
Norwalk
Stamford
Greenwich

Connecticut River
Quinebaug R.
Housatonic R.

MERRITT PARKWAY
WILBUR CROSS PKWY
TURNPIKE
CONNECTICUT
91
84
86
44
6
52
138
2
85
9
95
8
7
45
202
6
34

Connecticut

CONNECTICUT is known for the high quality of its antique shops and for its many fine craft shops and factory outlets. Most of the latter are located along the industrialized southern coast and between New Haven and Hartford. Excellent buys can be made at the many arts, crafts, and antique sales and festivals held in this state each year. The exact dates, times and locations of many of these events may be determined from an excellent, free, forty-page booklet that contains numerous color photographs and helpful travel information. This booklet, *Connecticut, So Much, So Near*, is available along with a state highway map and other travel information from the Connecticut Department of Commerce, 210 Washington Street, Hartford, CT 06106, telephone: 203-566-3385.

SOUTHWESTERN

- **BETHEL**. *J. Thomas Melvin Antiques* (The Pear Tree). 10 Wooster St. 203-744-5244 and 203-938-2620. Open Fri.–Sun. 12–5. Mr. Melvin carries a general line of furniture and household accessories, with the emphasis on period furniture, especially selected orientals. Recent offerings included a William and Mary kneehole desk, circa 1695 ($6,500), an eighteenth-century secretary-bookcase of Honduras mahogany ($14,000), and a pair of late Ming chests ($8,500). Mr. Melvin avoids collectibles and fads. His shop is in an eighteenth-century barn with hand-hewn chestnut beams.
- **BRANFORD**. *Annual Arts and Crafts Fair*. Bittersweet Farm. 203-488-9161. Early July. This annual fair attracts seventy-

five selected exhibitors of works in all media and several thousand visitors to the two-day event.

• **BRIDGEPORT**. *International Silver Company Factory Store*. International Silver Company., 315 Warren St. (University Square). 203-334-2890. Open Mon.–Sat. 9:30–5:30 and until 9 P.M. Thurs. This factory outlet sells silver flatware and hollowware, pewter, sterling, gold electroplate, and stainless flatware at discounts of 33⅓–60 percent off original or suggested retail price. The discount applies regularly on selected items, and in June there is a big annual clearance sale.

Levine's Factory Showroom. Mortimer, Allan and Howard Aaron. 27 Harrison St. (Connecticut Turnpike Exit 27A then exit at Main St.). 203-335-6468. Open Mon.–Sat. 9–5:30, Thurs. 9–8:30 P.M. The showroom offers 8 thousand square feet of nationally advertised name-brand fashion merchandise, current styles, first quality at a savings of 20 to 50 percent off retail prices. It carries moderate to better women's coats, suits, rainwear, sportswear, and dresses. There are special sales in January and June. The showroom is located in a turn-of-the-century factory building next to the factory which can be toured. Visitors can see how suits and coats are assembled.

Main Modes, Inc.—Leather Factory Outlet. 1225 Connecticut Ave. (opposite City Trust Bank). 203-366-3565. Open year-round Sun.–Fri. 10–3; closed Sun. in summer. The Leather Factory Outlet features leather and suede coats, jackets and sportswear for the entire family. All garments are manufactured on the premises and sold at wholesale prices. The savings are 50 percent and more.

Pappagallo Outlet. 1693 Park Ave. 203-333-3338. Open Mon.–Sat. 10–5:30. The Outlet features Pappagallo shoes, women's boots, and handbags at discounts of 30–75 percent off. In January and July the Outlet has special inventory sales too.

Seth Thomas Factory Outlet (see *Thomaston*). Seth Thomas Clock Company. University Square. Open Tues.–Sat. 10–5.

Strawberry Patch. 1718 Capitol Ave. 203-333-8850. Open Tues.–Sat. 10–5. The Strawberry Patch carries gifts and crafts for children and adults. They also have stationery. The store features pottery, wooden toys, and children's batik-dyed clothing.

• **CHESTER**. *One-of-a-Kind, Inc*. Tom, Cecile, Bob, Dot, and Oliver Perry. Chester Center (Rt. 9, exit 6). 203-526-9736. Open daily, evenings by appointment—call 203-526-9646. The Perrys carry a mixture of all kinds of antiques from Victorian to Primitive and accessories. They have desks, sets of chairs, tables, cabinets and demand items in good condition, many are unusual. The shop is located in historic Chester in an enormous two-story fieldstone building (1909) that was built by Italian immigrants as a feed and grain store and later was a silent movie theater. The second floor has 22-foot high ceilings with unusual pressed tin designs.

Betty and Walt Killam Oriental Art. 122 Middlesex Pike (Rt. 9A). 203-526-2967. Open 11–4 by appointment. The Killams specialize in true antique Oriental art. They carry Chinese porcelain, bronze, and furniture; and Japanese netsuke, swords, ceramics, scrolls, and prints. Betty Killam, known the world over as "Mrs. Netsuke," offers an outstanding collection of netsuke, ojime, and inro. The shop is in their home, an old farmhouse (1803). On the premises the Killams have cultivated a lovely Bonsai Garden.

• **DANBURY**. *Danbury Hat Company Factory Outlet Store*. 89 Rose Hill Ave. (exit 5 S off I-84). 203-743-2715. Open Fri. and Sat. only 9:30–4. The Hat Factory Outlet features headware: Stetson-Fur Felts, Westerns, Velours, Cloth Hats, Knitwear, and Caps. The hats are sold at discounts of up to 50 percent off retail price and special sales are run seasonally with discounts of up to 70 percent off retail.

Danbury State Arts and Crafts Fair. Danbury Fairgrounds. 203-748-3535. Mid-July. The State Arts and Crafts Fair displays the work of 300 exhibitors and attracts more than 30 thousand spectators.

• **DARIEN**. *The 1860 House of Darien*. 682 Post Rd. 203-655-8896. Open Mon.–Sat. 10–5. The shop is located in a charming nineteenth-century frame house on historic Boston Post Road. There are four rooms full of antiques, books, and collector's items. The books are for collectors (first editions, rare and out of print) and the other antiques are interesting and varied. The rooms contain iron and tin, woodenware, spongeware, quilts, country items and country and period furniture (all prior to the twentieth century).

● **DEEP RIVER**. *Luta Studios*. Giampiero and Nancy Mazzoni. Rt. 9A (exit 4 off Rt. 9). 203-526-5812. Open in the summer. Luta Studios carries crafts—all handmade—by Connecticut craftspeople. They offer hand-decorated tiles, figurines and functional and decorative pottery. There are also fiber arts, weaving, knitting, jewelry, macrame and quilts. The Mazzonis take custom made orders at the studio.

● **DERBY**. *Tiffany House Lighting Fixtures*. 304 Seymour Ave. (exit 17 off Rt. 8). 203-735-2050. Open daily 10:30–5. Tiffany House features hand crafted stained glass lamps and lighting fixtures and custom windows (made to order). There are discounts of up to 70 percent off list price and continual selections of close-outs as well as first-line merchandise.

● **ESSEX**. *Connecticut Mariner*. Capt. Alan L. Bish. 5 Griswold Square (opposite the Griswold Inn; exit 65 off Connecticut Turnpike). 203-767-8198. Open daily Apr.–Dec. and weekends Jan.–Mar. and by appointment. Captain Bish carries only antique and decorative nautical accessories. The shop, located in a nineteenth-century carriage house, features marine paintings, nautical books, navigation instruments, models, scrimshaw, and nautical antique lamps. Some recent offerings were: a large nineteenth-century ship's compass ($150), ship's globe lamp ($85), and a scrimshaw child's toy of a lady on a swing ($750).

James E. Elliott, Antiques. 8 North Main St. (just off the Square in Essex Village). 203-767-1600. Open Tues.–Sat. 11–4. Appointment suggested Jan.–Mar. Mr. Elliott offers Empire and Regency furniture, British pottery and porcelain, and Art Nouveau and Art Deco. He also carries Staffordshire in all its various forms and ABC plates and mugs.

● **GREENWICH**. *Alena Jewelers-Designers*. Alena Zinn. 12 East Putnam Ave. 203-869-0934. Open Tues.–Sat. 10–5. Alena specializes in simple, contemporary jewelry of which many items are made in her own workshop. The shop also carries some enameled jewelry in sterling and gold and creates a variety of jewelry that is fashioned with diamonds and other gems.

The Elements. 14 Liberty Way. 203-661-0014. Open Tues.–Sat. 10–5. Closed August. The shop offers contemporary crafts including functional and decorative pottery, fiber arts, enamelware, stoneware, jewelry, macrame, woodwork, carving, stained glass, metalwork, and blown glass. Among the craftspeople represented here are glass by Simpson, Correia, Carlson, Salamandra, and Ipsen; ceramics by Jay Lindsay, Linda Bottalico, Wilhelmi, and Wilenski; fiber by O'Shea, Foster, and Warner and jewelry by Arintzen, Besnard, and McLain. The shop was a long unused livery stable that was remodeled in 1974.

Estate Treasures Antique Center. Lillian London and Harriet Roughan. 1162 East Putnam Ave. Riverside (Rt. 1) (I-95, exit 5, one half block on left). 203-637-4200. Open Mon.–Sat. 10–5:30. The Center offers five antique dealers in one complex; there is sure to be something here for every taste. The shops carry English and American furniture, china, glassware, jewelry, objets d'art, fine paintings, clocks, and tools.

• **GUILFORD**. *Annual Guilford Handcrafts Exposition*. On-the-Green. 203-453-5947. Mid-July. This annual fair is sponsored by the Guilford Handcraft Center. It displays the works of a hundred selected exhibitors and attracts an audience in excess of 75 thousand.

• **HADDAM**. *Hobart House*. Malcolm Stearns, Jr. Saybrook Rd. (Rt. 9A). 203-345-2525. Open year-round by appointment. Hobart House is limited to pre-1830 antiques with specialties in antique silver and needlework. Recent offerings included a number of silver nutmeg graters dating from 1695–1825 ($150–$600), several silver wine funnels from 1760–1820 ($175–$575), a Peter and Ann silver tankard ($2300) and a large selection of antique needlework samplers from 1721–1835 ($65–$725). Hobart House was built in 1691 with a ballroom added in 1790 and is decorated with a large family collection of American furniture, Oriental rugs and English eighteenth-century porcelain (all of which are *not* for sale).

• **HAMDEN**. *Saxony Coat Company*. 1443 Dixwell Ave. (exit 60 off Rt. 15). 203-288-3600. Open daily 10–5:30. The Saxony Coat Company has been manufacturing fine women's coats for about three decades. The large retail outlet store on the premises offers coats from several well-known manufacturers at discounts of 20–40 percent off.

• **KILLINGWORTH**. *Old World Antiques*. At the Country Store. Rebecca and Lloyd Bergeron. Rt. 81. 203-663-2122. Open June–Aug. Thurs. and Fri. from 12–6, weekends by chance. This shop specializes in Victorian furniture as well as some country pieces and clocks. Recent offerings included a Victorian curio cabinet with five beveled mirrors and a heavy carving featuring a lion's head ($495), a Victorian oak dresser with three drawers and a mirror ($170), and a refinished three-drawer tool chest. This little shop has granite floors and a nice fireplace.

• **MADISON**. *Annual Original Madison Historical Society Antiques Fair and Flea Market*. Madison Green. 203-566-4210. This show and flea market is quite large and is held in late August.

Fence Creek Antiques and Collectibles. Annette and Bill Dane. 916 Boston Post Rd. 203-245-0151. Open daily 10–6. The Danes carry china, crystal, silver, pottery, old metals, and quilts. They also have antique clothing and decorator's items such as advertising tins and baskets. The shop is located in a yellow and white Cape Cod overlooking Fence Creek with its many resident marsh birds—herons, gulls, and ducks.

• **MERIDEN**. *Connecticut House Pewterers, Inc*. 122 Charles St. 203-634-0555. Open Mon.–Sat. 9–4, evenings Tues. and Thurs. 6–10 P.M. Closed Sat. June-Aug. The factory specializes in pewter holloware. This is spun pewter, a method dating back to the twelfth century and the most common since the seventeenth century. The company sells quality firsts and factory seconds at discount rates which they prefer not to publish. They also specialize in repairing and resilvering silver plated items.

International Silver Co. 500 Broad St. 203-634-2541. Open Mon.–Fri. 9:30–5:30 and Sat. 9:30–4. International Silver offers first quality and seconds of pewter, silver, and stainless holloware and flatware all at discounts of one-third off suggested retail or better. Special sales are held periodically, one in the spring, one in August, and one after Thanksgiving. Adjacent to the factory outlet is Heritage House, a four-room replica of New England life 200 years ago with a typical Georgian dining room, a pewterer's work-shop, a tavern scene, and a reproduction of an old silversmith shop. The entrance gallery contains authentic coin silver and pewter pieces from the late eighteenth century. Heritage House open Mon.–Sat. 10–3.

Rockwell Silver Company. 24 Randolph Ave. 203-238-7800. Open Mon.–Fri. 9–5. The factory manufactures sterling silver deposit on crystal and sells irregular items and first quality at 25 percent discount.

Silver City Glass Company Factory Store. 122 Charles St. 203-237-0429. Open Mon.–Sat. 9:30–5:30. The Factory Store is located in a nineteenth-century textile factory building. It sells sterling-on-crystal and gold-on-crystal plus all types of decorated glassware manufactured by Silver City Glass Company. The store offers discounts of up to 30 percent on Silver City items.

● **MIDDLETOWN**. *Annual Arts and Crafts Festival*. Xavier High School. Exit 11, off Rt. 9. 203-346-0320. End of April. This annual event is sponsored by the Middletown Junior Women's Club and attracts over 100 exhibitors in all media.

● **MILFORD**. *Juried Art Exhibition*. Milford Public Library. 203-878-6647. The Milford Fine Arts Council sponsors this annual exhibit of the works of 100–125 artists.

Milford Oyster Festival. Arts and Crafts Show. Milford Green. 203-878-4960. Late August. One part of this popular festival is the one-day arts and crafts show which attracts 150 exhibitors in all media and about 30 thousand spectators.

● **NEW CANAAN**. *Silvermine Guild of Artists, Inc*. 1037 Silvermine Rd. 203-966-5617. Open daily except Mon. 12:30–5. The Gallery features changing art exhibitions of paintings and crafts in all media including graphics. The shows change every three-and-a half weeks. The craft shop is open at all times and features nationally known craft people—blown glass goblets by Peter Bramhall of Vermont ($45), mohair and silk stoles woven by Libby Miller ($60) and a soup tureen by Joann Riley, including eight bowls and ladle ($60). The Guild features many special exhibitions and all member shows throughout the year, visitors can call for schedules.

One show that always receives particular attention is the annual New England Exhibition of Painting and Sculpture held for over twenty-five years in the month of June.

The Guild also sponsors a large *Christmas Exhibition* of all their craftspeople. The exhibition occupies all galleries and is held from Thanksgiving to Christmas Eve, annually.

● **NEW HAVEN**. *Peter Indorf Contemporary Design Jewelry*. 155 Park St. (Off I-91 or 95 near Yale's British Art Center). 203-776-4833. Open year-round Mon.–Sat. 10–5:30 and Thur. evening until 9 P.M. The shop features handmade custom jewelry with some unique designs in stock. The specialties are fine quality gemstones and jewelry of 14- and 18-karat gold and sterling silver.

● **NEW MILFORD**. *The Silo*. Ruth Henderson. Upland Rd. 203-355-0300. Open May 1 to Dec. 31 Wed.–Sun. 11–5. The Silo started as a country kitchen store. Later art gallery space was added where arts and crafts are exhibited monthly both for appreciation and sale. Recent exhibitions have included pottery (functional and decorative), furniture, graphics, paintings, stained glass, metal and wood sculpture, soft sculpture, fused glass, found metal sculpture, and rare wood decorative sculpture. The Silo is located in renovated twin silos, haymow, and adjacent barns.

● **NEWTOWN**. *Buttonshop Antiques*. Patricia Parker and Charles Bevensee. South Main St. 203-426-6698. Open year round, Sat.–Wed., 11–5. This shop specializes in Victorian antiques and accessories and Art Nouveau and Art Deco. Items include silver, china, glass, jewelry, and oak and walnut furniture. Recent offerings included an 18-karat Victorian gold ring with three opals and four small diamonds ($150), a five-piece sterling silver dresser set with embossed roses ($110) and an oak Larkin desk ($130).

● **NORWALK**. *Warren and Ruby Baur*. Silvermine Ave. 203-847-3310. Open by appointment only. The Baurs offer a general line of antiques and specialize in Victorian lighting devices such as a pull down electrified Victorian light ($225). They also carry primitives, tools, kitchen items, and glass.

Carolina Bed and Bath. Carolina Factory Outlets, Inc. 696 West Ave. 203-838-4106. Open Mon.–Sat. 9:30–6 and Wed. 9:30–9. This shop carries comforters, sheets, towels, blankets, shower curtains, bedspreads, bathroom rugs, and pillows from manufacturers such as Fieldcrest, Martex, Springmaid, and Bloomcraft. Prices are 30–70 percent off retail and all items are in stock year-round.

International Silver Co. 694 West Ave. 203-838-2301. Open Mon., Tues., Thurs.–Sat. 9:30–5:30, and Wed. 9–9. This factory outlet sells first quality sterling, silverplate, pewter, craftmetal, gold electroplate, holloware, and flatware. All merchandise is one-third or more off suggested retail prices.

Intimate Apparel Factory Outlet. Warner Slimwear. 618 Main St. (Rt. 7—exit 40 off Merritt Parkway, then 1 mi. north). 203-846-2488. Open Mon.–Sat. 9:30–5:30, Thurs. and Fri. until 9 P.M. The Warner Factory Outlet features women's intimate apparel (bras, girdles, briefs, bra-briefs and lingerie, gowns, etc.) at discounts of 50 percent off regular retail prices. They also sell discounted sweaters. There are additional markdowns throughout the year.

● **OLD SAYBROOK.** *Wilson's Antiques.* Jane Wilson. 1 Hammond Rd. 203-388-9547. Always open. Ms. Wilson specializes in eighteenth-century antiques and is an authority on Canton China.

● **ORANGE.** *Tri-City Coins–Antiques.* Tom Arnone. 222 Boston Post Rd. 203-795-4477. Open daily 10–6. Mr. Arnone specializes in old and new coins and currency and old clocks, pocket watches, and jewelry.

● **SANDY HOOK.** *Church Hill Galleries.* Dorothy Soloway. Church Hill Rd. (exit 10 off I-84). 203-426-9104. Open all year by appointment. Ms. Soloway specializes in period and primitive furniture, accessories and Folk Art of the seventeenth, eighteenth and early nineteenth centuries. The shop caters mainly to dealers. It is located in the Squire John Sanford House built c. 1773. Recently on sale was an early maple Tap Table with button feet and one drawer ($775).

● **SOUTH WOODBURY.** *Country Bazaar.* Jerry Madans. 451 Main St. (4 mi. north of I-84 exit 15 on Rt. 6). 203-263-2228. Open daily. The shop is located in an eighteenth-century carriage shop with hand-pegged beams. It offers a wide variety of antiques such as tools, all antique metals, prints, and paintings, crockery, primitives and memorabilia. Jerry Madans says he specifically avoids "barbed wire, beer cans, and Avon bottles!"

● **SOUTHPORT**. *The Keeping Room*. (inside Freedmans of Southport). Thomas Sheridan and Kerry Fuller. 2600 Post Rd. (Rt. 1). Open daily except Tues. and Sun., 10–5. The Antique Shop is incorporated in a retail furniture and design center. The shop carries American and English country furniture of the eighteenth and nineteenth centuries and has unusual antique accessories. It features interior design services.

● **STAMFORD**. *Couturier Galerie*. 1814 Newfield Ave. 203-322-2405. Open Mon., Thur.–Sat. 11–4. The Galerie features internationally renowned artists with special emphasis on Latin art and Israeli sculpture. A few of the artists represented here are Irma Mezey, Jaime Antunez, Sergio Gonzalez-Tornero, and Esteban. There are three major exhibitions a year. At Christmas the Galerie also carries crafts—weaving, hand-blown glass, and Haitian jewelry. The Gallery is located in a 100-year-old barn.

United House Wrecking. 328 Sellek St. 203-348-5371. Open Tues.–Sat. 9–5. United House Wrecking is one of Southern Connecticut's better known outlets. Here in 30 thousand square feet of buildings is an extraordinary collection of mostly salvaged house parts including doors, leaded glass windows, fireplace mantels, New York City subway signs, old beams, hatch covers, sinks and tubs, garden statues and virtually any other house or ground component from plain to fancy. In addition there are nautical items, imported brass and copper (old and new), butcher block tables, reproduction and original furniture, and French baker's racks (reproductions). Many times, special items such as old organs or a collection of early school bells appear. This is a browser's paradise. The selection is unbelievable, but don't expect unusual bargains; prices are typical and fair for the trade.

● **STRATFORD**. *Stratford Art Festival*. Sterling House to West Broad Green. 203-378-2606. Mid-June. This show is open to works in all media with crafts exhibits subject to selection by jury. The festival has attracted about 200 exhibitors and an audience of over 5 thousand in the past.

● **TRUMBULL**. *Professional Crafts and Arts Show*. St.

Joseph's High School. 203-929-4553. Late April. This invitational show features the drawings, paintings, photography, and crafts of sixty selected artists and craftspeople.

State Open Exhibit of Connecticut Classic Arts. Trumbull Library. Main St. 203-378-5891. April. This show attracts the work of 200 artists who display paintings, drawings, graphics, and sculpture throughout the month.

● **WATERBURY**. *Lil's Doll Hospital*. Lillian Baksa. 300 Wolcott St. (I-84, exit 23A). 203-754-9037. Open Mon.–Fri. 10–3 by appointment and chance. Ms. Baksa specializes in repairs of dolls, especially antique ones. Occasionally, she sells antique dolls.

● **WESTBROOK**. *Another Antique Shop*. H. and M. Frankel. West Pond Meadow Rd. (at Dennison Rd.). 203-399-7240. Open daily 10–5 or by chance. The Frankels' shop carries a general line of small antiques with special attention to primitive kitchen equipment, tin, copper, mirrors and early advertising ware. Recent offerings included a green, metal RR ticket box ($60), leather hi-hat travel case ($16), old copper ring mold ($20) and a World's Fair trylon/perisphere lamp ($75). Their shop is in a board and batten barn situated behind an eighteenth-century house on a country road. The shop was known for years as "Stuff for Sale." Inquire in advance for driving instructions.

● **WILTON**. *Vallin Galleries*. Peter Rosenberg. 516 Danbury Rd. (Rt. 7). 203-762-7441. Open daily except Wed. 11–5, and by appointment. Mr. Rosenberg carries only oriental art and antiques. Although his specialty is eighteenth-century Chinese porcelain and furniture, he also carries a broad range of oriental art from the tenth century B.C. to the nineteenth century including paintings, sculpture, textiles and bronzes. The shop is located in a 1719 saltbox on the Norwalk River.

● **WOODBURY**. *Forjay Farm Antiques*. Jean Jeske. Old Town Farm Rd. (3 mi. north of town, left off Rt. 6). 203-263-4135. Open weekends and holidays and by chance, 10–4:30. The Farm offers country home furnishings and decorating items of the eighteenth, nineteenth and twentieth centuries. It also carries country store articles. Ms. Jeske recently had a set of four plank seat chairs ($150), an 1865 wood washing machine ($100), and various small tables ($65–$90). The shop is located in a restored old barn across from an associated 1713 Saltbox.

Turn o' the Century Antiques. Rose and Walter Kurzmann. 434 Main St. 203-263-2829. Open Wed.–Sun. 10–6. The Kurzmanns offer both antiques and selected crafts in an 1880 Victorian house in the historic district of Woodbury. Their selections include unusual old wicker (Victorian, Edwardian, and Art Deco) both natural and refinished white; refinished oak furniture such as commodes, bonnet dressers, hall stands, sets of chairs, ladies desks, side-by-sides, and old clocks. They also offer original designs in stained glass mirrors, lamps, etc., tile tables and accessories, stoneware pottery and Batik hangings.

NORTHWESTERN

• **AVON.** *Gene and Jo Sue Coppa.* 20 East Woodhaven Dr. (7 mi. from exit 39 off Rt. 84). 203-673-3722. Open by chance or appointment all year. The Coppas specialize in country furniture and quality accessories of the eighteenth and nineteenth centuries. They carry an excellent selection of quilts, samplers, blue spongeware and baskets, and much more. They recently had a pair of brass andirons ($150) and a triple Irish chain quilt ($275).

Farmington Valley Arts Center, Inc. Avon Park North (on Rt. 44, 12 mi. west of Hartford). 203-678-1867. Open Wed.–Fri. 11–3, Sat. 11–4, Sun. 1–4. The Arts Center contains studios for twenty artists and craftspeople, and many of the studios are open to the public for retail sales several afternoons a week. The Gallery at the Center features changing exhibitions showing work of the resident artists. The media represented here are functional and decorative pottery, weaving, fiber arts, graphics, painting, jewelry, leather, stained glass, and sculpture. The Center is housed in nineteenth-century buildings formerly used to manufacture explosives. For over forty years the Society of Connecticut Craftsmen has held its annual Crafts Show here from mid-April to mid-May. Works to be exhibited by Society members are carefully selected by a jury.

• **BANTAM**. *Gooseboro Brook Antiques*. Carolyn Butts. Old Turnpike Rd. 203-567-5245. Open daily 11–5, appointment suggested in Jan. and Feb. This shop carries a complete general line with no specialty. Frequently Ms. Butts purchases entire estates as a means of maintaining diversity. Recent offerings included a large primitive oxen yoke ($275), an early decorated child's sled ($95), and a signed Heisey punch bowl with cups ($110).

• **BETHLEHEM**. *Ed Clerk Antiques*. RD #1 on Rt. 61 between Woodbury and Litchfield. 203-567-5093. Open by appointment only. Mr. Clerk specializes in Shaker furniture and accessories and carries some other very early New England country furniture and accessories.

• **BRISTOL**. *Bristol Chrysanthemum Festival*. Mum Festival Craft Fair. 203-583-1524. Mid-Sept. to early Oct. The Mum Festival is held annually in this town when the mums achieve their full brilliance on Chippen's Hill. The three-week festivities include parades, a tennis tournament, an 8-mile "mum-a-thon" race, a carnival and the Arts and Crafts Fair (held one weekend only—call for exact dates).

• **CORNWALL BRIDGE**. *Gunnar K. Holmes, Antiques*. (Junc. Rts. 7 and 45). Open daily 8–8, Sun. 10–6. The shop specializes in American furniture c. 1650–1850 and antique dolls 1850–1930. Mr. Holmes also carries paintings (American portraits and landscapes c. 1820–1880), clocks, folk art, samplers, and weathervanes.

• **FARMINGTON**. *Annual Farmington Crafts Expo*. Polo Grounds. First weekend in June. American Crafts Expositions, Rockport, Mass., sponsors numerous crafts fairs throughout New England including this one. Call or write Rudy Kowalczyk (P.O. Box 358, Rockport, MA 01966) for a complete listing. This annual event attracts 200 selected craftspeople.

• **GOSHEN**. *Tranquil Acres Antiques*. Jeanne Dautrich. North St. (the shop is on a private road off Rt. 63). 203-491-3716. May–Nov. daily 11–5 and weekends 12–6. Closed Tues. Mrs. Dautrich carries antique jewelry, glass, silver, and furniture. She also has tinware, cook books and a barn full of good used furniture.

The specialties are fine jewelry, coin silver and sterling, and old china. The shop is located in a 115-year-old ice house with later additions. It is situated on thirty-four beautiful acres of land.

● **HARTFORD**. *Connecticut Antiques Show*. Antiquarian and Landmarks Society of Connecticut. State Armory. Broad St. 203-566-4210. Early Oct. This is a large antiques show held for the benefit of the historic houses maintained by the society. The show is a three-day affair.

Full Moon. Aileen Dailey. 26 Union Place (across from the RR station). 203-247-5615. Open Mon.–Sat. 11–6. Aileen Dailey exhibits and sells pottery, batiks, wooden toys, weavings and stained glass by local artists. She will also take custom orders. In addition to the local crafts, Full Moon stocks imported crafts and decorative items from all over the world.

Greater Hartford Civic and Arts Festival. Constitution Plaza. 203-278-3378. Early to mid-June. This annual event attracts nearly 150 thousand spectators who can see and purchase the work of 500 exhibitors.

● **KENT**. *Bull's Bridge Glassworks*. Stephen and Joy Fellerman. Rt. 7. 203-927-3302. Open Spring–Christmas, Wed.–Sun. 10–5:30. Closed Feb.–Mar. Open also by appointment. Stephen Fellerman's art glass has been awarded many top prizes at shows throughout the country. His work appears at numerous invitational and juried shows and often is featured in interior decorator's magazines. The Glassworks carries Fellerman's functional and decorative blown glass, individually blown in the studio, signed and dated. He also makes rolled sheet glass on the premises (the glass may be purchased by stained glass artists). A small fee is requested in the studio section of the barn where visitors can watch the blowing. The gallery is free and carries not only Fellerman's work but occasional shows of photographs, paintings, and grandfather clocks.

The Victorian Shop. Elfriede Slason. Rt. 7. 203-927-3074. Open daily 10–5. The shop is located on the first floor of a Victorian townhouse and features a general line of antiques and collectibles. The specialities are tools, glass, and furniture. Recently the shop featured an Empire Sofa ($350) and a Peach Blow Pitcher ($295).

• **LITCHFIELD**. *Annual Litchfield Arts and Crafts Show and Sale*. Litchfield Jr. High School. 203-567-5737. Early October. This show is held for one weekend and is sponsored by the Litchfield–Torrington Auxiliary Child and Family Services. The show attracts the works of seventy artists and craftspeople in all media who have been selected by a jury of professionals.

Harry W. Strouse, Antiques. Maple St. (off Rt. 202). 203-567-0656. Open daily 9–5, call first. Mr. Strouse carries a general line of country and formal antiques, including furniture, china, glass, textiles, tools, pewter, silver, brass, copper, prints, paintings, rare books, samplers, rugs, fireplace equipment, wrought iron, and religious items. Recent offerings included an early Sheffield silver-plated ink stand, Matthew Boulton, ca. 1784 ($200), a pair of eighteenth-century brass andirons ($200), and a country style tripod tilt and turn birdcage table ($500). Mr. Strouse avoids Victorian, Art Nouveau, Art Deco, reproductions, and collectibles. The shop is located in a 1749 house overlooking the Litchfield Hills with an "Indian Well" in the basement and hand-hewn, pegged beams in the attic.

• **MARBLEDALE**. *Don Abarbanel*. Rt. 202, opposite St. Andrew's Church. 203-868-2436. Open May–Oct. daily except Wed. 11–5 and by appointment. Mr. Abarbanel carries antiques and decorative objects of the eighteenth and nineteenth centuries. He offers Delft, English pottery, Indian miniatures, quilts, and books on antiques and collecting. Recently the shop featured an Art Nouveau, French walnut breakfront with burl veneer, attributed to Louis Majorelle.

• **NEW HARTFORD**. *Waring Factory Outlet Store*. Waring Products. Rt. 44. 203-379-0731. Open Mon.–Fri. 9–3:30. The Outlet Store features Waring Electric Appliances at discount prices. For example, blenders that retail for $25.99 are sold for $17.92. There are also specials at bargain prices and a special two-day warehouse sale on Saturday and Sunday in early December each year.

• **NEW PRESTON**. *Woodville Antiques*. Mr. and Mrs. Frederick D. Smyth. Valley Rd. Woodville (Rt. 202 to Rt. 134 west then first right). 203-868-2523. Open by chance or appointment: July and Aug. daily 9–7 P.M; other times, weekends and evenings. The Smyths specialize in early American country antiques with the emphasis on a large collection of old tools and primitives. They carry much woodenware, wrought iron and early kitchenware, such as early tin, pewter, copper and earthen ware. The shop recently had a small pine kitchen cabinet ($35), a chestnut country Sheridan table ($60), wrought iron utensils such as forks, ladles, and cleavers (from $10 up) and tools (from $1 up).

• **PLAINVILLE**. *Cookie Jar Antiques*. Cookie Bartosewicz. Plainville Railroad Station Antique Flea Market (permanent booths). Rt. 72 (exit 34 off I-84 west on 72 to town). 203-747-9094 weekends; 203-747-1018 weekdays. Open every Sat. and Sun. 9–5 all year and by appointment. Cookie carries a complete general line of antiques and quality collectibles. Her speciality is an extensive stock of Depression Glass. The shop recently had a set of five Heisey Crytolite Swans ($85), a mahoghany curio with doors and mirror ($200) and a large selection of Railroad items and postcards. This shop is one of ten shops housed in the *Old Railroad Station*.

Plainville Railroad Station Antique Flea Market. Rt. 72 (exit 34 off I-84 west on 72 to center of town). 203-757-1018 weekends. Open every Sat. and Sun. 9–5 year-round. The Flea Market contains ten permanent antique shops. They are housed in the *Old Railroad Station* (1908) by the tracks, where the freight trains add a little thrill as they rumble by. In this nostalgic setting the shops are located in the Ticket Master's Room, Baggage Room and in the nooks and crannies.

The Railroad Flea Market sponsors an annual antiques show and sale, which attracts thirty-two dealers, on the grounds of the old station. The show is held in late Aug.

• **RIVERTON** (Hitchcocksville). *The Antique Shop of Elizabeth Winsor McIntyre*. Rt. 20 in the center of town. 203-379-4726, 203-379-0846. Open all year daily, 11–5. Now this is a shop with something for almost any antique lover! Here are ten rooms chock full of wonderful antiques of all sorts and sizes: Each of the rooms is different—one has old dolls, toys and antique infants' and little girls' clothing; another, pine furniture; and yet another, "turn of the century" kitchen with iron stoves, accessories, enamelware, copper, etc. As Ms. McIntyre says "I specialize in *not* specializing!" Recently she had a Tiger Maple Schoolmaster type Desk ca. 1800 ($1700) and butter paddles ($2–$40). The shop is located in Riverton (home of Hitchcock Chair), a "walking" town with the Hitchcock Museum, dozens of restored nineteenth-century homes, four antique shops, an herb shop and a Pewter Craft Shop and more. It is well worth a visit!

The Catnip Mouse—Luncheon and Crafts. Bobbi and Dryden Clark. Rt. 20. 203-379-7274. Open all year Tues.–Sat. for luncheon and in the summer for late afternoon tea. The crafts offered at the Catnip Mouse include theorems (the 1800s art of stencil painting on velvet), soft sculptured pictures, quilts, pillows, dolls, placemats, blockprinted notepapers, napkins, three dimensional reverse paintings on glass, Suffield candies, pottery, and stuffed catnip mice. The shop and restaurant is located in an early nineteenth-century Greek Revival style house built by Pelatiah Ransom in 1840. Many rooms retain the original wide board floors.

Governor Cooke House Antiques. Warren H. Webster. Main St. 203-379-4003. Open daily in summer 10–5; winter—Tues.–Sat. 11–4. Although this shop has a general line of antiques, collectibles, memorabilia and gifts, it is most representative of Empire and Victorian antiques. Recent offerings included an Empire chest with original brass ($250) and a plant stand with original gold leaf ($75). The shop has six antique-filled rooms in a Victorian house built in 1880 by the Governor of Connecticut.

Sarah Hubbard Putnam—Antiques and Herbs. Rt. 20. Open all year Tues.–Sat. 11–4:30 and by appointment. Ms. Putnam has an attractive shop in historic Riverton. She carries an excellent line of Victorian furniture and has some small pieces of silver. She offers a few primitives and nice old baskets. Recently there was a lovely rosewood piano stool c. 1853 ($275) and a Gout stool (rosewood and needlepoint) ($175). Her daughter makes herb teas which visitors may purchase; plants are available for purchase in the spring. Be sure to ask to see the selection of cards Ms. Putnam sells; they are very popular.

Seth Thomas Factory Outlet (see **Thomaston**). Seth Thomas Clock Co. Rt. 20. Open Tues.–Sat. 10–5.

- **SALISBURY**. *Undermountain Weavers*. Lottie and Eric Gerstel. Undermountain Rd. 203-435-2321. It is a good idea to call before arriving—the Gerstels are often there on Fridays and Saturday and on and off during the week. This is a studio workshop where fine wools from the Shetland Islands and rare Chinese cashmere are woven by hand on century-old Scottish handlooms. The wonderful lightweight fabrics are designed for suits and skirts, scarves and ties. The Gerstels will arrange tailoring. They also sell custom built handlooms and give weaving instruction: call for information on classes.

- **SIMSBURY**. *Hawkshead Antiques*. Lawrence A. Foster. 56 County Rd. (1 mi. from Rt. 10 and Rt. 202). 203-658-9841. Open in winter weekends 10–5; summer—daily 10–5 by chance or appointment. Hawkshead carries only country Americana and period accessories. It has one of the most extensive stocks of American iron in New England. The furniture specialty is old cupboards. Mr. Foster recently carried a New Hampshire corner cupboard, old blue, c. 1825 ($1250) and an eighteenth-century toddy iron ($110). The irons range from $5 to $500.

  C. Russell Noyes. 9 Hopmeadow St. (Rt. 10, 1 mi. north of Avon). 203-658-5319. Open most days by chance. Closed Jan. 4–March 15. Mr. Noyes offers a fine line of antique furniture, both formal and informal, woodenware, copper, pewter, and many unusual small items. He does not carry china and glass. He recently had a wonderful Chippendale slant top desk ($2450) and a cherry bow front chest ($975). There is a nice collection of pine country furniture in modest price brackets.

- **SOUTHINGTON**. *Apple Festival*. 203-628-8036. First two weekends in October. This event includes an arts and crafts fair in addition to the food booths, parade and other activities sponsored by the Southington Chamber of Commerce.

- **THOMASTON**. *Seth Thomas Factory Outlets*. Seth Thomas Clock Co. 135 South Main St. 203-283-5881. Open Tues.–Sat. 10–5. Seth Thomas has been making clocks since 1813. The factory outlets have bargains on thousands of irregular and discontinued clocks.

- **TORRINGTON**. *Barredo's Antiques and Used Furniture*.

Joseph and Evelyn Barredo. 2496 S. Main St. (Rt. 8 exit 42—½ mi. on right on Old Torrington Rd.) 203-482-0627. Open all year, Tues.–Sat. 10–5:30. The Barredos buy entire estates, so their stock is widely varied. They handle antiques, collectibles, and memorabilia. The shop carries oak, cherry, clocks, horse carriages, coffee grinders, desks, china, glassware, brass, and jewelry. They have brass beds (from $100 up). Recently they featured a 5-foot-tall store coffee grinder dated 1873 ($1000), and a hand carved Senate desk ($3000).

Early Attic Shop. Jean and Mike Tomasiewicz. 1188 New Litchfield St. (Rt. 202 east of Litchfield Center). 203-482-9991. Open Wed.–Sun. 11–5 and by appointment. This shop carries antiques and a line of mahogany reproductions. The furniture includes a selection of primitive and Victorian pieces. Also featured are tinware, cut glass, pewter, copper, brass, and china. Recently there was a dry sink c. 1760 ($495) and arrow back chairs c. 1820 ($75 each).

● **UNIONVILLE**. *C. W. House Factory Store*. Cascade Wooden Mills (see *Oakland, ME*). 19 Perry St. 203-673-2518. Open all year Mon.–Sat. 9:30–4:30. The Factory Store features discounted prices on Wool Fabrics: solids, plaids, tweeds, tartans, coordinates, and woven polyesters. They sell Billiard cloth, pressed felts and remnants, seconds, and pound goods.

● **WEST CORNWALL**. *Martin Gold, Books and Antiques*. Rt. 128. 203-672-6333. Open daily 10–5 and by appointment. This is one of the largest second-hand and rare book shops in New England. It also carries a large selection of antiques and collectibles which are housed in the same building. The shop is strong in Americana, paintings, and prints. Martin Gold has primitive and Victorian furniture, paper ephemera, advertising art, tools, and household utensils. The shop recently had a cradle ($200), a painting by Douglas Volk ($1500) and a turn-of-the-century highboy ($900). European furniture and paintings are avoided here. The shop is housed in an old Masonic Hall. The two-story building is wood frame with wainscott construction.

● **WEST HARTFORD**. *Spring Arts and Crafts Festival*. West Hartford Armory. 203-623-0520. Early May. This show is sponsored by the New England Artists and Craftsmen's Guild and includes works in painting, graphics, drawing, sculpture, and crafts by sixty selected exhibitors.

EASTERN

• **CANTERBURY**. *Stone of Scone Antiques*. Jeanette Stratton. Corner of Water St. and Bingham Rd. 203-546-9917. Open all year, weekdays 12–dark and weekends, 10–dark. This shop carries antique furniture—specializing in Victorian Oak, children's furniture, and pine. There are also several lovely old quilts—all made before the year 1900. Recently Ms. Stratton had a c. 1850 whale's tooth with scrimshaw on both sides, a c. 1840 homespun coverlet (red and white linen and wool), and a small leather covered hand-painted trunk c. 1830.

• **COBALT**. *Arthur Collins Antiques*. Jct. Rts. 66 and 151 (halfway from Portland to East Hampton, CT). 203-342-1144. Open daily 10–5:30. Mr. Collins carries New England furniture, oriental rugs, silver, paintings and prints, and antique lights.

• **COVENTRY**. *Caprilands Herb Farm*. Mrs. Adelma Grenier Simmons. Silver St. (short drive off Rt. 44A, between Manchester and Willimantic). 203-742-7244. Open Apr.–Dec. 9–5, and 1–5 Jan.–Mar. Although we have strived to keep this listing as impartial as we could, it is just not possible in the case of Caprilands. Mrs. Simmons is one of those special persons that only rarely enter one's life. Not only is she one of the country's foremost herbalists, but she manages to share her knowledge and enthusiasm for herbs in so many special ways. The farm itself is a treasure, centered around a 200-year-old red-brown clapboard house filled with hundreds of herbs, spices and dried floral arrangements and herbal wreaths. It is here that Mrs. Simmons conducts her famous herbal luncheons (Monday through Friday, April through December, reservations needed). The grounds have numerous carefully planned herb gardens with ornamental and edible herbs grown to their best advantage in both formal and informal arrangements. Mrs. Simmons has recently overseen the complete restoration of the 200-year-old barn on the property which will now provide further storage, display and shop space for the business. Herbs and other plants may be bought here as seeds, young plants, dried products or in wreaths and other arrangements. Mrs. Simmons is always happy to answer any and almost all questions.

The Old Country Store. Barbara and Burton Baver. 1140 Main St. (Rt. 31) 203-742-9698. Open Tues.–Sun. 10–5. This large assemblage of antiques, collectibles and memorabilia is housed in two buildings on opposite sides of the street—the Old Country Store itself which was built in 1784, and an old Methodist Church, built in 1848. In all there are ten rooms of antiques. The general line includes virtually every sort of item (with the exception of paintings and rare books). Recent offerings included an 18 in. Kestner character baby doll ($325), a black walnut drop-leaf table ($85) and an Elgin Key Wind Watch ($58). There are 59¢ grabbags and an as-is shelf with items from $1–$6. Lots of fun exploring at this shop with its original slanted counters, designed for the convenience of women in hoop skirts.

• **EAST HADDAM**. *L'Atelier Antiques and Interiors*. Raymond and Diane Cummings. Main St. (jct. Rts. 82 and 149). 203-873-9198. Open Thurs.–Sat. 11–5 and by appointment. The Cummingses specialize in eighteenth- and nineteenth-century American antiques and decorative accessories. The shop is located in a nineteenth-century Stage Coach Tavern and features such items as Windsor chairs ($20–$1200), a Chippendale chest of drawers ($1600) and nineteenth-century paintings ($100–$2500).

• **EAST KILLINGLY**. *Peep Toad Mill*. Sandra and Richard Farrell. Peep Toad Rd. 203-774-8967. Open to the public for group shows twice a year (Labor Day Weekend and Thanksgiving Weekend) and by appointment. The Farrells make and sell their own pottery in a wonderful old stone and wood mill located on an unpaved country road by a scenic millpond with a two-arch stone bridge over it. Peep Toad Mill is an excellent example of a very early New England Textile Mill; the Farrells have converted it into living quarters, studio, and crafts gallery. The group shows featured here include work by the Farrells and local professional craftspeople—Wayne Rundell, baskets; Judy Branfman, weavings; and Robert Lucas, pottery. Other artists in a variety of media are included in the show by invitation. Peep Toad's Labor Day Show spills out of the gallery into the garden beside the mill, where foods of the season are available.

• **EASTFORD**. *General Lyon Inn Antique Store*. Adjacent to the inn. 203-974-1380. Open daily except Monday. Call ahead in the winter months. This small shop is part of the Bowen family business that includes the running of the lovely old *General Lyon Inn*. The Bowens carry a nice line of general antiques that include baskets, some furniture (primitives through Victorian), depression glass, china (eighteenth- to late nineteenth-century), textiles, kitchen ware, and woodenware. They do not carry mission oak furniture and its accessories. In addition to the antique line they carry herbs (dried and plants) from their own herb garden and offer herb dinners with lectures at the inn (phone for current schedule). They also carry the line of Crab Tree and Evelyn imported English preserves.

• **HEBRON**. *Hebron Harvest Fair*. Rt. 85. September. This popular agricultural fair includes an Arts and Crafts Show in addition to the usual tractor and horse pulls, livestock and poultry judging, pie eating and nail-driving contests.

• **LYME**. *Lyme Art Association Spring Show*. Lyme Art Association Gallery. Lyme St. 203-434-1291. Memorial Day through mid-June. This show has been held for over 50 years each spring.

Old Clocks. Charles M. Murphy. Rt. 156. 203-434-1052. Open daily, 9–5. Mr. Murphy specializes in the sale and repair and restoration of early New England and French clocks. Recent offerings included a Daniel Burnap cherry cased tall clock ($13,000) and a Waltham Jewelers Regulator, mahogany and glass ($2,750). Mr. Murphy avoids German, Japanese, and contemporary clocks.

• **MANCHESTER**. *Bezzini's Old Colony Company*. 596 Hilliard St. (call for driving instructions). 203-649-3183. Open Mon.–Sat. 8–5. Old Colony is a manufacturer (since 1929) of upholstered living room furniture—sofas, loveseats, chairs, swivel rockers and sleepers. All of these are available at the outlet at savings of up to 60 percent off list price. The factory and outlet are in the old Hilliard Mills that were established in 1794 as an early woolen mill. Blankets were made at this mill for the soldiers of the War of 1812 and the Civil War.

Foot Prints Inc. (a nonprofit community center). 466 Main St. 203-643-8953. Open Mon.–Sat. 10–5 all year. The Center exhibits and sells arts and crafts of Connecticut artists. Housed in an old red brick church building, the Gallery exhibits changing shows of various art media, each with its own theme—crafts, photography, soft sculpture, weavings, or paintings.

- **MARLBOROUGH**. *Festival of Creative Arts*. Blish Memorial Park. 203-295-9971. Late September. This two-day event attracts about 120 artists and craftspeople each year.

- **MOODUS**. *Down on the Farm, Ltd.* The Simon family. Banner Rd. (follow signs from Moodus Center). 203-873-9905. Open in spring and summer Tues.–Sat. 11–6, Sun. 12–5. Fall and winter—Tues., Wed., Sat. 11–5, Thurs. and Fri. 11–8, and Sun. 12–5. Closed Mondays and Jan.–April 10. This is an interesting and unique craft center. There is a retail craft shop and gallery selling fine quality handcrafts in many different media. Over 100 professional craftspeople are represented in the shop. The Simons carry functional and decorative pottery, original design furniture, weaving, fiber arts of all sorts, enamelware and cloissone, stoneware, jewelry, leather, woodworking, stained and blown glass, metalwork, quilts and pillows, batik, handmade brooms, kitchen utensils, and toys of all sizes and mediums. The craft shop is located in a restored chicken coop and is part of a larger craft center with resident craftspeople in adjoining studios. The center was the brainchild of the Simon family and is located on a working poultry farm.

L. Peck—Antiques. Louis and Lillian Peck. N. Moodus Rd. 203-873-8782. Open by appointment or by chance, calling first is recommended. This shop carries antiques, collectibles, memorabilia, and gifts, including new quilts in many sizes. Among their offerings are carnival glass, cut glass, Heisey glass, mustache and shaving mugs, Nippon, Austrian, and Bavarian pieces, tables, chairs, lamps, oil lamps, large and small pictures, framed prints, china, and some silver and brass.

• **MYSTIC**. *Annual Mystic Outdoor Art Festival*. Downtown Area. 203-536-9644. Mid-August. This annual event attracts almost 500 exhibitors who may not display work until it has been screened. Work includes painting, drawing, sculpture, photography, and graphics. This event usually attracts over 50 thousand spectators.

• **MYSTIC SEAPORT**. *Mystic Seaport Museum Store*. Mystic Seaport—nonprofit educational organization. Rt. 27, exit 90 off I-95, 1 mi. south. 203-536-9688. Open all year, 10–5. Museum admission not required for the store. One of the largest stores dedicated to maritime gifts and crafts. The huge rambling houselike building has loads of nooks and crannies filled with merchandise to discover. The Wheel Room features antiques and unique maritime furniture such as hatch-cover tables and ship's wheels. There is an area dedicated to scrimshaw jewelry and old and antique scrimshaw artifacts. The Country Store has old fashioned candies, jams, and jellies; another area contains solid brass lamps, door-knockers and candlesticks. Upstairs is the famous Seaport Book and Print Shop. The Museum Shop sells hand-woven rugs ($55) made by museum weavers, and hand-built ship models ($300–$2,000).

• **NEW LONDON**. *Annual Flea Market*. Ocean Beach Park. Second Saturday in May.

Hempstead House Antiques. Ward Young. 110 Hempstead St. 203-447-2311. Open by appointment. The shop specializes in American and English furniture, Oriental porcelains and unique antique objects. Recently Mr. Young had a Connecticut cherry tilt-top table with board top ($495) and Ko Imari Porcelains (from $45 to $450). The shop is located in a restored 1840 Victorian Italianate Villa near historic New London seaport and the historic Hempstead House.

• **NORTH GROSVENORDALE**. *North Grosvenordale Foam Rubber and Shoe Outlet, and Quinn's Shirt Shop*. Robert L. Fiander II. Rt. 12. Shoes: 203-923-2981, shirts: 203-923-2589. Open Mon.–Sat. 10–4, all year. These two shops under the same roof and the same management offer Arrow and Enro shirts (seconds) and Bostonian shoes (seconds and overstocks) discounted at approximately 40 percent off list price. The shops are in a 150-year-old brick building that was originally the employees food store associated with the Cluett Peabody Mills nearby.

- **NORWICH**. *Annual Exhibition of Work by Connecticut Artists*. Converse Art Gallery, Slater Museum, Norwich Free Academy. 103 Crescent St. Late March through late April. This juried show of paintings, graphics, sculpture, and crafts has been held for more than thirty years and always attracts several thousand visitors.

- **OLD LYME**. *My Grandmother's Attic Antiques*. Sandra-Lee Buckley. 30 Mile Creek Rd. 203-434-8166. Open by appointment. The shop carries a line of antique country furniture and furnishings. There are baskets, wooden ware, upholstered buggy seats and wing chairs upholstered in crewel fabric. Featured were a Queen Ann style wing chair upholstered in crewel ($400) and a variety of baskets ($15–$60).

Pfeiffer Cloisonne. Andrew and Marianne Pfeiffer. 132 Whippoorwill Rd. (5 mi. from exit 70 on I-95, call for specifics). 203-434-5621. Open by appointment. The Pfeiffers' studio is located in their home where they handle only their own original work—fine handwrought cloisonne enamels—jewelry, boxes, and wall pieces. They also do wax castings of silver, again Pfeiffer original designs. The cloissonne jewelry ranges from $60 to $1000; the silver-castings jewelry, from $20 to $100; and the collectibles (boxes, etc.) sell at $25 and up.

- **OLD MYSTIC**. *Stone Cellar Antiques*. Beverly Thayer. 126 Route 27 (off I-95, west 1 mi.). 203-536-4344. Open most weekends and by chance. The Stone Cellar carries mostly primitive and country antiques of furniture, iron, tin and pottery. Ms. Thayer recently had a beautiful blue and white woven coverlet ($85) and an 1840 chestnut blanket chest ($90). The shop is located on the first floor of a quaint half-stone, half-wood, center chimney Colonial built in 1790.

- **POMFRET CENTER**. *Meadow Rock Farm Antiques*. Don and Georganna Dickson. Rt. 169. 203-928-7896. Open most of the time. The shop carries country and primitive antiques and a selection of hand-crafted gift items. The Farm is located in an old barn on the site of the old Pomfret Golf Course.

• **SALEM**. *Annual Autumn Antique Show*. Gardner Lake Firehouse. Rt. 354. 203-536-1641. (New England Tourist Information Center). This Antique Show is held early in October.

• **SCOTLAND**. *Devotion House Antiques*. Lillian and Don Glugover. Rt. 97. 203-456-0452. Open by appointment or chance. Devotion House specializes in American antiques prior to 1840 and folk art. The period furniture and accessories are both country and formal. They recently had a Gov. Winthrop desk in maple c. 1780 ($2200) and a mahogany kitchen cupboard c. 1840 ($575).

• **SOMERS**. *Paul's Carriage Shed*. Paul A. Bray. South Rd. (Rt. 83). 203-749-6926. Open Sun. 10–5 and anytime by appointment. Paul features antique wood, iron, depression glass, crocks and carpenter's tools from the 1800s. He has an extensive collection of over sixty wood mortars and pestles. Recently there were five roll-top desks in the shop ($600 each).

• **UNCASVILLE**. *The Pants Pocket*. Fay Levine. 150 Norwich–New London Turnpike (Rt. 32). 203-848-1445. Open daily 10–5:30. Closed Sun. This is an outlet store featuring slacks and accessories for men and women. The slacks are sold at wholesale prices; they are manufactured at the Levine's factory— the Majestic Trouser Co., Inc.

• **VERNON**. *Greater Vernon Annual Arts and Crafts Fair*. Vernon Center Middle School. 203-871-1888. Mid-November. This juried show of paintings, drawings, graphics, sculpture, and crafts includes the work of a hundred selected craftspeople and artists and attracts an audience in excess of 10 thousand.

• **WAUREGAN**. *Wauregan Mills Fabric Store, Inc*. Walnut St. 203-774-8491. Open Mon.–Thurs. 10–9, Fri. 10–6, Sun. 11–6; closed Sat. This outlet carries designer sportswear for men and women at 40 percent or more off retail prices. Designers include Jones, N.Y.; Diane von Furstenberg; Pierre Cardin; Ralph Lauren; Christian Dior, and more.

Massachusetts

MASSACHUSETTS offers shoppers a fine year-round selection of shopping opportunities thanks to the diversity of its vacation places that range from the seacoast to the Berkshire Mountains. For the convenience of readers, we have divided the state into four primary geographical shopping areas—Western, Central, Eastern, and Cape Cod. Readers are reminded that the emphasis of this series of books is on rural New England and will therefore find relatively more listings away from the Boston suburbs. Within each area, the listings are alphabetical by town.

Before leaving on your trip we recommend writing for some general travel information available from the Massachusetts Department of Commerce and Development, Division of Tourism, Box 1775, Boston MA 02105. 617-727-3205.

WESTERN

Helpful, free travel information is available from Berkshire Vacation Bureau, 205 West St., Pittsfield, MA 01201 and from the Pioneer Valley Association, 333 Prospect St., Northampton, MA 01060.

- **ADAMS**. *Old Stone Mill Outlet*. Rt. 8. 413-743-1015. Open Mon.–Fri. 10–4, Sat. 9–12 noon. This outlet handles seconds and discontinued lines of hand-printed and machine-printed wall coverings, featuring traditional designs as well as some contemporary ones. Many of the papers are available with correlated fabrics. The

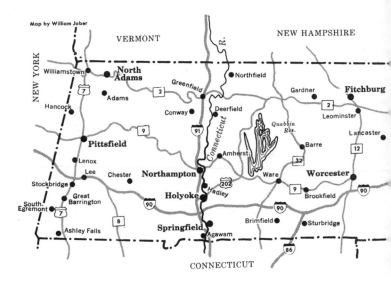

Map by William Jaber

VERMONT   NEW HAMPSHIRE

NEW YORK

Williamstown   **North Adams**
                                  ● Northfield
        Adams   Gardner   **Fitchburg**
                      Greenfield   2
Hancock   Leominster
              Conway   ● Deerfield
                                        Quabbin   Lancaster
                                        Res.
        Pittsfield   9   12
                                              ● Barre
            Lenox   ● Amherst   32
          Lee   Chester   **Northampton**   Ware   **Worcester**
Stockbridge   202   90
              Great   **Holyoke** Hadley   9   Brookfield
South-   Barrington   90   90
Egremont   7   Brimfield ● Sturbridge
        Ashley Falls   8   **Springfield**
                                  Agawam   86

CONNECTICUT

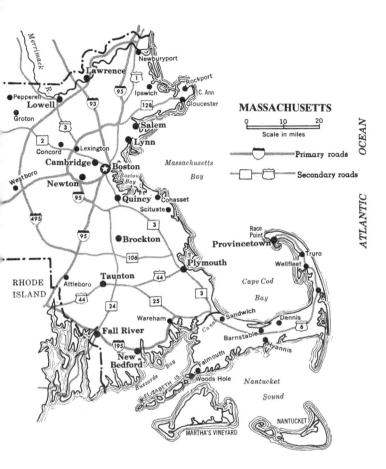

MASSACHUSETTS

Scale in miles

0 — 10 — 20

Primary roads

Secondary roads

RHODE ISLAND

ATLANTIC OCEAN

Massachusetts Bay

Boston Bay

Cape Cod Bay

Nantucket Sound

Buzzards Bay

MARTHA'S VINEYARD

NANTUCKET

ELIZABETH IS.

Merrimack R.

Newburyport
Lawrence
Pepperell
Lowell
Groton
Ipswich
Rockport
C. Ann
Gloucester
Salem
Lynn
Concord
Lexington
Cambridge
Boston
Newton
Westboro
Quincy
Cohasset
Scituate
Brockton
Provincetown
Race Point
Truro
Wellfleet
Plymouth
Taunton
Attleboro
Dennis
Wareham
Sandwich
Fall River
Barnstable
Hyannis
New Bedford
Falmouth
Woods Hole

discounts on these products vary from 50 to 80 percent off regular retail price. This shop does custom printing for interior decorators as well as the manufacture of their nationally distributed lines. Visitors may watch both the hand-printing and machine-printing operations in this old stone mill building, which was built in 1830 and was once a water-powered weaving mill.

● **AMHERST**. *Eastern Mountain Sports*. Rt. 9, Amherst–Hadley Line. 413-253-9504. Open Mon.–Fri. 9:30–9, Sat. 9:30–5:30. See *North Conway, NH* for more information.

R. and R. French, Antiques. Rachel C. French. 657 South Pleasant St. (Rt. 116 south 1 mile; just before bridge take E. Hadley Rd. for 100 ft.). 413-253-2269. Open daily by chance or appointment. Rachel French offers eighteenth- and nineteenth-century antiques, furniture, pewter, fireplace equipment, china, primitives, and textiles. She does not carry clocks. Recently the shop had Lemon andirons with matching tools ($450); a 15 in. Badger pewter charger ($550) and an English 9½ in. pewter plate (Edgar) ($75). The shop is located in a gambrel-roofed eighteenth-century house.

The Wood-Shed—Antiques. Harlan A. Woods, Jr. and Beatrice L. Woods. 156 Montague Rd. (Rt. 63) 413-549-1720. Open Mon.–Fri. (it is best to call first) by chance or appointment. The Wood Shed sells antiques and collectibles. The Woods feature primitives and have metal and wooden wares, ironstone and campaign memorabilia. They do not carry furniture. Recently the shop had a N.Y.C. Railroad Lantern ($25), a spinning wheel ($75) and a large round chopping bowl ($40).

● **BRIMFIELD**. *Brimfield Antiques*. Richard and Susan Raymond. Main St. (jct. of Rts. 19 and 20, 6 mi. west of Sturbridge). 413-245-3350. Open summers Mon.–Sat. 10–5 and Sun. 1–5; all other times by appointment. Brimfield Antiques carries only American furniture made prior to 1840, both country and formal with accessories of the same period. Some of the articles include andirons, samplers, paintings, candlesticks and other forms of lighting. The Raymonds do not deal in firearms or coins. The shop is currently in the town's original general store, on the common.

Reid's Famous Flea Market. Main St. Three Saturdays each year. 413-245-3333. This very popular series of flea markets draws about seven hundred dealers and crowds of from 10,000 to 15,000 spectators each time they are held—usually in mid-May, July, and September. Call the above number for the exact dates and more information.

• **CHESHIRE**. *Cheshire Village Antiques*. June and Gustave Nilson. South St. (Rt. 8). 413-743-4385. Open daily except Mon., June 1–Oct. 31, 10–6. The Nilsons carry a general line which includes antiques, collectibles and memorabilia. Their specialties are country, painted, and Shaker furniture; Americana and folk art.

• **CONWAY**. *Conway House*. Jack and Ray VanGelder. Rt. 116–Ashfield Rd. 413-369-4660. Open all year by chance or appointment. This shop offers a complete line of country antiques from the eighteenth and nineteenth centuries. The shop stresses primitives, early lighting devices, iron, brass, copper, tin and glass objects, and English and American samplers. In addition the shop has china, furniture, paintings, and a nice selection of early accessories including quilts and coverlets.

• **GREAT BARRINGTON**. *Wonderful Things Inc.* 232 Stockbridge Rd. (Rt. 7). 413-528-2473. Open 10–5 daily, Sun. 1–5. Closed Wed. Jan.–Mar. This is a complete craft center—a mini mall of six shops in one building. They sell over 30,000 items including crafts supplies, finished crafts and hobbies. There are seven rooms which serve as living quarters, eight for working, and ten rooms are open to the public. The shops represent over 300 professional craftspeople, mainly from the northeast. Craft supplies are offered in almost all media and there are January sales by department and clearance sales all year.

• **HADLEY**. *Metamorphosis*. Robert A. Berra. 206 Russell St. (Rt. 9). 413-584-8810. Open Tues. Sat. 10–5:30, other times by appointment. This shop handles antiques only and specializes in furniture of all kinds, ranging from early country pieces, through Empire and Victorian, up to and including turn-of-the-century golden oak. Recent offerings included a pine cupboard or bookcase with glass doors, bracket base, and original red and yellow paint ($94); a Victorian walnut oval-back lady's chair ($335); and a golden oak rectangular library table with one drawer, refinished ($120). Mr. Berra does not sell any furniture "in the rough." He specializes in restoration which includes repairs and refinishing of antique furniture.

Skera. Harriet Rogers. 123 Russell St. (exit 19 off I-91, right onto Rt. 9). 413-586-4563. Open Tues.–Sun. 11–6, Thurs. and Fri. until 9 P.M. Skera carries only American handcrafts, both functional and decorative. The prices range from $1.75 to $2,000. There is a selection of ceramics, jewelry, glass, weaving, wood crafts, and batik. The gallery is located in a large yellow house built in the 1800s. In August, Skera features an annual clearance sale.

● **LANESBORO**. *Amber Springs Antiques*. Larry and Gae Elfenbein. 29 S. Main St. (Rt. 7). 413-442-1237. Open daily, year-round. Amber Springs is a general line store with offerings that include country American furniture, pottery, china, glass, porcelain, advertising art, toys, utensils, tools, pewter, brass, copper, tin, silver, clocks, primitive paintings, Christmas tree decorations and Shaker items. They avoid reproductions, jewelry, stamps, coins, guns, and other weapons, and Oriental antiques.

● **LENOX**. *Crazy Horse Antiques*. Charles L. Flint. Main St. 413-637-1634/243-9835. Open June–Sept. daily, Oct.–May Mon.–Wed., Fri., Sat. 10:30–5 and by appointment. Charles Flint specializes in Shaker antiques and also carries primitives and good American furniture. He has some rare American decorative items and a collection of folk art. The shop is located in a handsome colonial brick plaza in the center of beautiful Lenox.

● **LEVERETT CENTER**. *Leverett Craftsmen and Artists, Inc*. Montague Rd. 617-549-6871. Open daily 12–5 except Christmas, Thanksgiving, and New Year. This shop carries the crafts and arts produced by craftspeople and artists that generally live within a 40-mile radius of the shop. Their selections include functional and one-of-a-kind pottery, original design furniture, weaving, graphics, painting, jewelry (including enamel on sterling and cloisoné, leatherwork, macrame, stained glass, traditional blacksmithing and blown glass. Leverett Craftsmen and Artists is located in a turn-of-the-century cheesebox factory, which later served as a chicken coop prior to renovation as a crafts and arts center. The center also gives a great many classes in a variety of crafts and arts media. Write for details.

The crafts center sponsors an Annual Fall Show in October. Call the center for details.

- **NORTHAMPTON**. *Dwyer's Bookstore, Inc*. Jeffrey Dwyer. 44 Main St. (1 mi. off I-91 at jct. of Rts. 9 and 5). 413-584-7909. Open Wed. and Thurs. noon–5:30, Fri. and Sat. 10–5:30, and by appointment. Dwyer deals in used and rare books. He carries used books in every field, rare books in the history of printing, typography, and literature, and books about books and related art fields. There are *no* paperback books or magazines. The third floor of the building contains an art gallery specializing in contemporary graphics and some photography.

Sutter's Mill. John and Cynthia Sutter. 233 Main St. 413-586-1470. Open Tues.–Sat. 10–5. Sutter's Mill exhibits and sells hand-crafted 14-karat gold and sterling silver jewelry, individually crafted diamond settings, and a selection of functional stoneware and pewter. Among the offerings are sterling silver earrings by Ed Levin with garnet stone ($12); 14-karat gold post earrings with opal by Levin ($45); a 14-karat gold diamond ring setting by John Sutter ($120)—the stone is extra; stoneware decanter and goblets by Dave Robinson ($45). The store received a preservation award from the Northampton Historic Society.

- **NORTHFIELD**. *The Carriage Stop*. Dot and Gil Gillmore. 166 Main St. 413-498-2810. Open April through December daily except Thursday. Also by appointment (call 617-544-3885). The Gillmores carry a general line but concentrate on primitives and country furniture. They also create their own lampshades and lamps. Recent offerings included a dovetailed jelly cupboard ($225), a watchmaker's chest ($225) and a grained blanket chest ($135).

- **PELHAM**. *Home Farm Antiques*. Anne L. Berra. 108 Amherst Rd. (3.5 mi. east of town). 413-253-3452. Open by appointment or by chance year-round. Ms. Berra carries a general line of antiques which include specialties in Staffordshire china, prints, silver, copper, and brass. Recent offerings included a rare,

Staffordshire brandy dispenser from a Victorian pub, in working order and with brass spigot ($120), a pair of coin silver tablespoons, c. 1835 ($34 pair) and a pair of cut glass salt dishes ($20 pair). Her shop is located in the loft of an old barn with hand-hewn, pegged beams dating from the early nineteenth century.

● **PIONEER VALLEY**. *Annual April Antique Show and Sale*. April. The Pioneer Valley Antiques Dealers Association sponsors this annual event. For details as to exact date and location as well as a list of all members of this association write: Mrs. F. Pugliano, Secretary, Pioneer Valley Antiques Dealers Assoc., P.O. Box 244, Westfield, MA 01085.

● **SHEFFIELD**. *Dovetail Antiques*. David and Judith Steindler. Rt. 7. 413-229-2628. Open daily except Tues. from 10–6. The Steindlers carry a line of American antiques that includes American eighteenth- and nineteenth-century country furniture, some accessories (glass, wood, brass, and ironware) but with the definite emphasis on American clocks. Especially important to them are nineteenth-century American clocks and the restoration and repair of clocks. This shop specifically avoids oak and wicker furniture.

Lawrence Goldsmith Antiques. Rt. 7. 413-229-6660. Open daily all year 10–5 and by appointment. Lawrence Goldsmith carries American furniture, both country and formal, of the eighteenth and nineteenth centuries. He also has folk art, paintings, pewter, silver, iron, copper and brass antiques. The shop recently had some signed Windsor chairs, signed American pewter, and a fine collection of eighteenth-century American silver.

Twin Fires Antiques and Arcade. Berkshire School Rd. and Rt. 41. 413-229-8307. Open Dec.–May, Mon.–Sat. 10–4; May–Nov. Mon.–Sun. 10–4. This very large shop contains six floors and a dozen shops full of antiques which are largely imported from England and France. Specialties include stripped pine furniture, brass, copper, stripped iron accessories and some French furniture. The selection here is very large and quite diversified within the limits described.

● **SOUTH EGREMONT**. *Gladys Schofield*. Rts. 23 and 41. 413-528-0387. Open Mon., Wed.–Sat. 11–5. Sun. 1–5. Also by appointment. Gladys Schofield has been selling antiques for twenty-

UNITED
House Wrecking

— 30,000 square feet of buildings —

THE JUNKYARD WITH A PERSONALITY

328 Selleck Street, Stamford, Conn. 06902 • Call (203) 348-5371

Closed Sundays & Mondays

6 acres of antiques, imports, relics and reproductions.

Leaded glass by the carload.

Doors, mantels and other architectural pieces from old buildings.

Tiffany style and oil lamp reproductions.

Left, scrimshaw *(Connecticut Mariner, Essex, CT)*; Right, rocking chair *(Old World Antiques, Killingworth, CT)*; Below, Sheffield inkstand made by Matthew Boulton, ca. 1784 *(Harry W. Strouse Antiques, Litchfield, Ct)*.

Above, pewter plates, goblets, and candlestick *(Connecticut House Pewterers, Inc., Meriden, CT)*; Left, wall clock *(Old Clocks, Old Lyme, CT)*; Right, two French dolls and a country cousin *(The Antique Shop of Elizabeth Winsor McIntyre, Riverton, CT)*

Above, two very different rosewood stools *(Sarah Hubbard Putnam—Antiques and Herbs, Riverton, CT)*; Right, miniature carving by Charles F. Murphy *(The Sneak Box Studio, Concord, MA)*

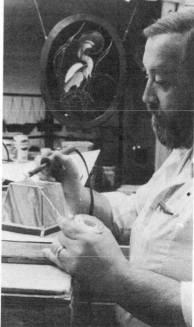

Above, high-temperature wheel-thrown majolica teapot with sugar and cream dispensers (*Eden— Hand Arts, Dennis, MA*); Right, John Knight working with glass (*The Glass Eye, North Eastham, MA*)

Antique wooden furniture
*(Crazy Horse Antiques,
Lenox, MA)*

Above, wooden truck by Matthew Temple *(Leverett Craftsmen and Artists, Inc., Leverett, MA)*; Left, 36-inch-high weathervane of repoussé copper *(Travis Tuck Studio, Vineyard Haven, MA)*

Shop interior *(Waterfall Antiques, South Dartmouth, MA)*

Delft bowl *(Sturbridge Village Museum Gift Shop, Sturbridge, MA)*

Shop interior *(Robert Thomas Antiques, Williamstown, MA)*

The Fantastic Umbrella Factory, Charlestown, RI

Right, farm and greenhouse products on display (*Hickin's Mountain Mowings Farm and Greenhouses, Brattleboro, VT*)

The Old Mill Craft Shop, Jericho, VT

Ceramics and silver pendants *(The Craft Shop at Molly's Pond, Cabot, VT)*

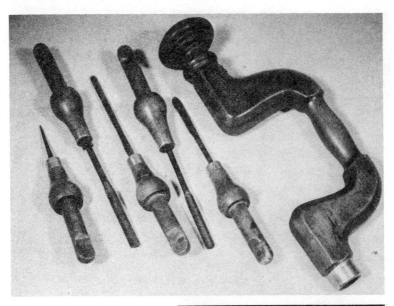

Above, primitive American bit brace with set of matlching bits *(Iron Horse Antiques, Inc., Poultney, VT; photo: V. Ward)*; Right, A work by the potter Jean Paul Patnode *(The Stowe Pottery, Stowe, VT)*

nine years at the same location—a lovely old white clapboard home built before the 1800s. She deals in a general line of antiques which includes collectibles and memorabilia. The shop features glass, china, clocks, mirrors, lamps, and eighteenth- and nineteenth-century furniture and paintings. The specialities here are lamps, custom lamp-shades, and unusual accessories.

• **SOUTH HADLEY**. *Annual Peddler's Fair*. Chapin Auditorium. Mt. Holyoke College. 413-538-2362. December. The college sponsors this annual show of juried works from New England and New York craftspeople.

• **STOCKBRIDGE**. *Annual Berkshire Crafts Fair*. Monument Regional High School. August. This fair is now in its fifth year and is becoming one of the most important juried fairs in the northeast.

Folklorica. Ellen and Don Gross. Main St. (in the Mews). 617-298-4436. Open daily in July and Aug. 10–6; weekends in spring and fall. Folklorica is a "folk art galleria and jewelry emporium." The specialty is unusual jewelry and objets d'art, including ethnographic, antique, contemporary, oriental, and Art Deco styles. Ellen and Don Gross feature hand-crafted mirrors ($7–$20); Art Nouveau necklaces ($7–$12) and one-of-a-kind antique Chinese necklaces ($75–$90). Some of the jewelry in the gallery is the work of Laurel Birch and Ed Levin. The shop is in a courtyard next to the famous Red Lion Inn.

Image Gallery. Clemens Kalischer. Main St. 413-298-5500. Open Mon.–Sat. 10–5. The Image Gallery deals in fine arts and crafts. There are paintings, sculpture, graphics, photography, and crafts (one of a kind) in various media. The gallery is located in an 1884 Dutch-style brick building with vaulted brick ceilings with iron beams and a tower. It was formerly the Town Office building.

• **WARE**. *Fredric's Knitted Fabrics, Inc*. Francis and Marjorie Byron. Ware Industries Mill Yard 413-967-5631. Open Mon.–Fri. 9–5, Sat. 9–12. This outlet offers sweaters, underwear, and hosiery at reduced prices. Sweaters are 30 to 50 percent off regular price. The store is located in an old New England stone mill that is 130 years old. Also in this old mill are the Ware Knitters who offer knit fabrics and shirts, Ware Factory Shoe outlet, Ware Sportware (skirts, slacks, and jackets), Rindge Industries (the

Wedgemoor woolens Mill Store), and the Diaper Bin (disposable diapers, paper towels, and other paper products).

Ware Metal, Inc., Remnant Nook. Off East St. (on Rts. 9 and 32, east of town). 413-967-6276. Open Mon.–Fri. 8–4:45 and Sat. 8–11:45. The Remnant Nook is located behind Sibley's Hardware Store. The store sells remnants of knits, cottons, pile fabric, sheeting, quilting, and diapers.

● **WEST SPRINGFIELD**. *Wel-Shoe Company* (see *Manchester, NH*). 1111 Riverdale St. (Junction of Rt. 5 and I-91). 413-739-0765. Open Mon.–Sat. 9:30–5:30, Thurs. and Fri. until 9 P.M.

● **WILLIAMSTOWN**. *Robert Thomas Antiques.* 115 Water St. (Rt. 43) 413-458-4747. Open all year, daily 10–6 except when at antiques shows. Mr. Thomas limits his offerings to American antiques with special emphasis on seventeenth- to early nineteenth-century formal and country furniture in its original paint, quilts, baskets, stoneware, folk art, paintings, and early glass. The only imported items are some Oriental rugs. With the exception of the above-mentioned slightly later furniture, nothing in his shop is post-1850. Among his more recent selections were an eighteenth-century walnut linen press ($6500), a set of seventeenth-century trestle foot andirons ($475), a splay leg tavern table ($650), and a nest of three Shaker oval boxes ($195). The shop is in his restored c. 1854 house.

CENTRAL

● **ATHOL**. *House of Burgess Antiques.* 62 Summer St. (directly off Rts. 2A, 7, 32, and 202). 617-249-4625. Open daily by chance or appointment. Mrs. Burgess specializes in ruby stained pattern glass and other colored Victorian glass. The shop also offers a general line of antiques, memorabilia and collectibles including china, small primitives, and old tools. She avoids large pieces of furniture and reproductions.

● **BROOKFIELD**. *The Seraph.* Sally and Valentin Dzelzitis. Rt. 148 (7 mi. north of Old Sturbridge Village). 617-867-9353. Open by chance or appointment. The Seraph offers architectural and interior design services, specializing in primitive antiques and fine reproductions. Valentin Dzelzitis, an architect, develops designs based on authentic antiques. Originally these sofas, chairs, cupboards, and chandeliers were designed for their 1731 saltbox, the John Watson House. The Seraph sells primitive antiques and Oriental rugs and designs and constructs custom reproduction furniture from measured drawings. The country sofas and wing chairs are advertised in *Yankee* and many of the antiques magazines and are found in many restored historic homes.

• **DUDLEY**. *Evergreen Farm Wool Shop*. Henry Easterbrooks. Oxford–Dudley Rd. 617-943-1371. Open year round, but it is best to phone before going to the shop. The Wool Shop carries sheepskin products such as coats, capes, vests, toys, footwarmers, hats, and mittens. The clothing ranges from very small children's to men's sizes. Also sold are just the sheepskins which can be used as throws on furniture and car seats or as rugs.

• **GARDNER**. *The Factory Store, Inc*. L. and Z. Kamman Furniture Factory. 88 Mechanic St. (jct. of Rts. 2 and 68). 617-632-2401. Open Mon.–Sat. 9–5. The Factory Store sells Kamman furniture at discounts of 50 percent and more. The brand-name merchandise in both colonial and traditional styles includes dining room, living room, bedroom, and occasional furniture in maple, pine, cherry, etc. A large heavy pine grandfather rocker, made in the Kamman factory, which sells retail for $205, is $89 here. The factory has been manufacturing furniture in this plant since 1852; it is an excellent example of a mid-nineteenth-century factory complex.

• **GREENFIELD**. *Red Barn of Greenfield*. Howard J. Arkush. 95 River St. (I-91, exit 26 east, turn right at the first traffic light). 413-773-7225. Open all year Mon.–Sat. 9–5 and other times by appointment. The Red Barn offers eighteenth- through twentieth-century furniture and glass. The shop recently had a cherry and butternut six-leg drop leaf table, an eighteenth-century maple tall chest, and sets of Sheraton and Hitchcock chairs.

• **NEW SALEM**. *Federal House Antiques*. Thomas Hutchinson. South Main St. (in the center of town). 617-544-6158. Open daily by chance or appointment. Thomas Hutchinson offers a general line of antiques and collectibles including furniture, china, glass, and coin silver. He recently had a rod back Windsor side chair ($67), an oil on wood painting (both sides) ($135), eight honeycomb egg cups ($95), and a forty-six piece porcelain tea set, English, unsigned ($97). The Federal House was built in 1810.

• **NORTH OXFORD**. *North Oxford Mills*. Bernard Edinberg. Clara Barton Rd. (1.4 mi. south on Rt. 12 from the jct. of Rts. 12 and 20 near the Auburn–Oxford line). 617-987-8521. Open all year, Mon.–Sat. 9–5, Wed. until 9 P.M. During July and August the store closes at noon on Saturday. This old factory building was built before 1878. It features custom braided rugs at 30–60 percent savings. You can see the women working at the machines and tables turning out rugs that range in size from $2' \times 3'$ to $12' \times 15'$. In addition to the rugs, the factory carries over 200 rolls of brand name carpets, rugs, and padding.

• **NORTHBORO**. *Basketville*. 200 Hudson St. Open daily, year-round. See *Putney, VT* listing.

• **PEPPERELL**. *Pioneer Homestead Antiques*. Virginia Aceti and Sheryl Duquette. 91 River Rd. (Rt. 111). 617-433-6221. Open daily 10–5 by appointment or by chance. This shop carries a full line of eighteenth- and nineteenth-century antiques, large and small, including country furniture and accessories, some Victorian, and Shaker collectibles. The proprietors avoid what they consider "flea market" items. This shop is in an attached, renovated carriage house.

• **PETERSHAM**. *Annual Antiques Show and Sale*. Town Hall. 617-724-6649. First or second weekend in October. This two-day annual event, now in its seventeenth year, is sponsored by the Petersham Unitarian Alliance.

• **SOUTH DARTMOUTH**. *Waterfall Antiques*. Betty Monjeau. 849 Rock-O-Dundee Rd. 617-636-8319. Open 12–5 daily except Sunday. This shop is 5 miles due south of exit 18 on I-95 in the village of Russell's Mills, next to the waterfall. Waterfall Antiques carries a complete line of antiques, furniture, china, quilts, and paintings in seven rooms that are located in a former barn. Typical selections at this shop included an antique rope bed, ball and bell turnings, maple, c. 1820 ($200), a mahogany drop leaf table, c. 1840 ($150) and a windmill pattern quilt ($65).

• **STURBRIDGE**. *Grandmother's Toys*. Betty Winslow, Wayside Shoppes. Rt. 20 at Arnold Rd. (west from town). Open

Apr.–Dec. 24, 10–5, Jan. 1–Mar. 12–4 weekends (weather permitting). Betty Winslow, "Grandmother," designs and makes dolls and soft toys and carries other crafts on consignment. She operates the shop herself and works on the dolls where customers may watch; children are especially interested in the construction. Among the dolls are storybook dolls (including the wonderful Little Red Riding Hood, Grandmother, Wolf doll), puppets, and marionettes. The other crafts are in a variety of media.

Sturbridge Village Museum Gift Shop. Sturbridge Village. 617-347-3362. Open daily except Christmas and New Year; winter 10–5, summer 9–6. The Sturbridge Village Museum Gift Shop offers a selection of carefully made reproductions of museum items from the Village collection. Among the types of items offered are colonial reproductions of glass, textiles, pewter, woodenware, tin, pottery, furniture (made as exact copies by the Kittinger Co.), brooms, and foodstuffs—grains, chowders, beans, and puddings. Wearing apparel made from textiles woven in the Village shops is available, as are hand-dipped candles (especially bayberry), and a number of forms of ironware including wrought iron, fireplace tools, hinges, and other building hardware items.

Sturbridge Yankee Workshop. Route 20. 617-347-9500. The Yankee Workshop is one of New England's largest and finest suppliers of reproduction furnishings including clocks, lamps, furniture, glassware, pewter, mirrors, and sconces. In addition to its stores in Sturbridge and Ipswich, Mass., the workshop has one of the most extensive and widely distributed, mail-order catalogs.

● **UXBRIDGE**. *Stanley Woolen Company Mill Store*. Arthur and Phil Wheelock. 140 Mendon St. (Rt. 16). 617-278-2451. Open Mon.–Sat. 9–5. The Mill Store sells designer woolen goods at prices below wholesale. They also discount imported and domestic yarns for weaving, knitting, and crocheting. The imported brushed wool yarn regularly $24 a pound is $16 a pound here and the $12.95 a yard wool fabric is only $6 a yd. Special sales are announced by a mailing list which customers sign at the store.

This business has been owned by seven generations of the Wheelock family, since 1810. The woolen mill, one of the few left in New England, is still in operation in the back of the store.

● **WORCESTER**. *Annual Worcester Crafts Fair*. Craft

Center, 25 Sagamore Rd. 617-753-8183. May. The Craft Center is a membership organization of over 1200 craftspeople. The center sponsors this important juried show annually; it is open to USA resident craftspeople.

EASTERN

• **BOSTON**. *Boston Crafts Show*. Hynes Auditorium. 617-536-0300. September and December. The Boston Crafts Guild, 29 Newbury Street, Boston, MA 02116 sponsors two annual juried crafts shows at Hynes Auditorium each year. The September show is their annual open show and the December show is the Christmas Antiques and Crafts Show and is invitational.

Eastern Mountain Sports. 1041 Commonwealth Ave. 617-254-4250. Open Mon.–Fri. 9–9, Sat. 9–5:30. See *North Conway, NH* for information.

Society of Arts and Crafts. 175 Newbury St. 617-266-1810. Open year round Tues.–Sat. 10–5. This is one of the oldest crafts outlets in the country. This distinguished gallery sells almost every conceivable form of contemporary craft including functional and decorative pottery, furniture, weaving, spinning, fiber arts, jewelry (one of a kind and limited production), wooden accessories, clothing, leather, blown glass, quilts, stained glass, macrame, and metalwork. The Society provides a number of special exhibitions each year including the Winter Show sponsored by the Massachusetts Society of Craftsmen and held during November and December. Call for exact dates.

• **BOSTON AREA**. *Annual Antique Show and Sale*. Suburban Antiques Dealers Association. Late April–early May. This show, now in its tenth year, is under the sponsorship of the Suburban Antiques Dealers Association. To receive information about the exact dates and times of the three-day show, write Ruth Berg, 228 Hayden Rowe, Hopkinton, MA 01748, and request a list of current members of the association. This listing also gives the dates and location of the show.

- **BURLINGTON**. *Wood Carving Exhibition*. Burlington Mall. May. The work of a great many carvers is displayed at this annual event under the sponsorship of the New England Wood Carver, Inc., Box 156, Lexington, MA 02173. 617-272-8867. This show has been held each year since 1970.

- **CAMBRIDGE**. *Ten Arrow Gallery/Shop*. 10 Arrow St. 617-876-1117. Open Mon.–Sat. 10–6, Thurs. 10–9. Ten Arrow is considered by many craftspeople to be one of the outstanding crafts outlets in the Northeast. Crafts are carefully selected by the owner from a wide variety of media and include decorative and functional stoneware, porcelain, jewelry, wood furniture and accessories, weaving and other textiles, fiber sculpture, blown glass, leather, enamels, metal holloware, and metal sculpture and much more.

- **COHASSET**. *Annual Craft Exhibition and Sale*. Cohasset Common. July. This fair is sponsored by the Cohasset Village and Harbor Assoc., c/o Ann Hamilton, 19 Elm St., Cohasset, MA 02025. The juried show has been an annual event since 1972.

- **CONCORD**. *The Catseye*. Richard J. Borovicka. Independence Center. 617-369-8377. Open Tues.–Sat. 9–5. The Catseye offers hand-made jewelry and gifts. The shop carries gold and silver jewelry and precious and semiprecious stones. The jewelers will repair jewelry and reset stones. The Catseye is located on the first floor of a turn-of-the-century firehouse.

The Sneak Box Studio. Charles F. Murphy. 101 Commonwealth Ave. 617-369-8312. Open year-round Mon.–Sat. 10–6. The Sneak Box Studio is a working studio of bird carver Charles F. Murphy. Decoy carvings are sold and Mr. Murphy gives classes in carving and painting. The studio also sells antique decoys, decoy books, decoy patterns, carving blanks, antique paraphernalia, and sporting prints.

- **FAIRHAVEN**. *Antiques and Interiors*. Martha L. Crowley. 115 Green St. (exit 24 off Rt. 195 east to Rt. 240 to town). 617-992-1389. Open daily 11–5 and by appointment. Martha Crowley offers elegant mahogany furniture (period and custom) and accessories. She also carries collections of general antiques. There are paintings and prints, brass, glass, silver, and rugs. Ms. Crowley is an interior decorator who specializes in the antique line. The shop is located in a fine old nineteenth-century sea captain's home which she has completely restored. The antiques are displayed in the roomlike settings. The town of Fairhaven is a very lovely old seaport town.

• **FALL RIVER**. *Fall River Knitting Mills*. Mill Store. 69 Alden St. 617-678-7553. Open Mon.–Fri. 9–9, Sat. 9–5. This old nineteenth-century textile factory offers sweaters at discounted prices. The sweaters are name brands, sold in specialty stores across the country, and are up-to-the-minute fashions. They can be custom trimmed with braid or trim to your own design here at the mill—making it a one-of-a-kind original.

Pick and Save Discount Shoe Outlet. Factory Outlet Center. 1637 North Main St. (Rt. 195 east to Rt. 79 north, take North Main St. exit). 617-675-2967. Open Mon.–Fri. 9:30–9, Sat. 9:30–5. The Outlet features men's and women's famous brand shoes at factory outlet prices—a minimum of 25 percent off retail prices.

• **HAVERHILL**. *Savoy Luggage Outlet*. Ward Hill Industrial Park. (Ward Hill exit off I-495). 617-374-0351. Open Mon.–Fri. 9–4:30. The outlet sells Savoy luggage and attache cases at discounted prices.

• **LAWRENCE**. *Bedspread Mill Outlet*. Matthew Frauwirth. 244 Broadway. 617-685-2303. Open Mon.–Sat. 9:30–5. This mill outlet sells first-quality bedspreads, draperies, comforters, and blankets at 50–60 percent below retail (some savings are on closeouts). Brands carried include Bates, Normandie Bedspreads, Springmaid, Everwear, and others. Special sales, held periodically, feature unusual buys on some firsts, closeouts and selected seconds at even greater savings.

• **MANSFIELD**. *Collectors Anonymous*. A consignment shop. 70 North Main St. 617-339-8066. Open Wed.–Sat. 10–4:30 and by chance or appointment. The shop handles all sorts of antiques, collectibles, and memorabilia. The collection is eclectic, reflecting the diverse tastes of the consignors. The only items specifically avoided are guns, Nazi items, and Avon bottles. The shop is located in a nineteenth-century carriage house attached to the Greek Revival townhouse.

• **MARLBOROUGH**. *Wayside Country Store*. Anthony and

Joan Scerra. Rt. 20. 617-481-3458. Open all year daily except Thanksgiving, Christmas, and New Year's Day 10–5:30. This old country store was once located in the center of Sudbury where it housed the post office for the village. When Henry Ford purchased the building while he was developing the Wayside Inn property, he had the store cut in half and moved to its present location (not far from Wayside Inn) by oxen. In the main building, the store has two floors. The first floor contains the general store with pickle barrels, a cheese counter and out-of-the-bin shopping including tinware, teas (more than fifty), bulk spices, jellies. The main floor also has the restored original old post office with many names of early Sudbury residents. The bake shop on this floor features the home baking (on premises) of breads, cookies, Congo bars, and other desserts. Upstairs at the shop is a large Colonial gift shop featuring pewter, glass, and other gifts. Also upstairs is the lamp shop which not only sells lamps but has one of the largest selections of globes, shades, and chimneys for old lamps in the area. Next door to the main building is the penny candy store with over two hundred types sold in old-fashioned bulk jars. A small restaurant serves breakfast, lunch, and ice-cream. Phone the store for driving instructions.

• **MARSHFIELD**. *South River Primitives*. Karel and Willis Henry. 22 Main St. (next to the South River at jct. Rts. 139 and 3A). 617-834-7774/834-4530. Open by chance or appointment. The Henrys offer early American furniture and accessories of the eighteenth and nineteenth centuries in the original finish and condition. The furniture is mostly early New England country and the accessories are folk art including quilts, needlework, weathervanes, paintings, watercolors, and pottery. They recently had a rare New England Press Bed in original red and in pristine condition ($950), an unusual Queen Anne Chair with arms in salmon red ($625) and an 1830 Family Register Watercolor in original grained frame ($325). The Henrys are usually off looking for the unusual and the unique in early Americana so they are rarely in their shop; a call ahead is strongly suggested.

• **MATTAPOISETT**. *The Corner Shop*. Doris and Al Winterbottom. 122 Fairhaven Rd. (Rt. 6). Shop: 617-758-4324; home:

996-9014. Open year-round 10–5 (closed Tues.) and by appointment. The Corner Shop carries a wide range of general antiques, changing constantly. There are lamps of all kinds, furniture in a variety of woods and wicker, old tools, glass (pattern, cut, depression) and china. The Winterbottoms have excellent collections of unusual collectibles and memorabilia. Just about the only things they do not carry are coins, jewelry, and newer items. Their shop is famous locally for the antique Steiffe Bears that sit outside in nice weather. They are not for sale!

● **MILFORD**. *Anthony Roberts, Inc*. The Graci Family. 45 Sumner St. 617-473-1422. Open Mon.–Sat. 9–5. The Factory Outlet sells all-weather coats for men and women at discounts of 40 to 50 percent off retail prices.

● **NEEDHAM HEIGHTS**. *Calvert's Inc*. 938 Highland Ave. (exit 56W off Rt. 128). 617-444-8000. Open Mon.–Fri. 9 A.M.–10 P.M. and Sat. 9–5:30. This is an outlet store carrying many brands and a variety of merchandise for the entire family at reduced prices. There are closeouts, discontinued items, and irregulars. Especially featured are Carter's clothing for children.

● **NEW BEDFORD**. *Brookside Antiques*. Louis O. St. Aubin, Jr. 24 North Water St. (just off Rt. 195). Open all year Mon.–Sat., 10–5, evenings by appointment. Brookside Antiques offers glass, china, and Victorian decorative items. There is a large stock of Mt. Washington and Pairpoint glass, Pairpoint Lamps, and cut glass. Mr. St. Aubin also features Victorian nineteenth-century art glass. He does not carry collectibles, paper goods, depression glass, Beams bottles, or new plates. The shop is in a 1790 whaling captain's house behind the Whaling Museum.

Clover Bay. 102 North Front St. 617-999-1255. Open Mon.–Sat. 10–5, Thurs. until 9 P.M. Clover Bay manufactures women's sportswear for major stores throughout the country. They sell the same first quality merchandise in the outlet store at 40 percent off retail price. There are special sales of even greater discounts in January and July.

Fairhaven Corporation Factory Outlet. 358 Belleville Ave. 617-993-9981. Open Mon.–Fri. 9–3:30, Sat. 9–2. The factory outlet sells ladies' handbags well below regular retail prices. They also have occasional sales when goods are marked down even farther.

Knapp Shoes. 251 Brook St. 617-994-2002. Open Mon.–Wed., Sat. 9:30–5:30, Thurs. and Fri. 9:30–9. This shop is a factory outlet for men's dress, work, and casual shoes. Typical savings: dress shoes that normally retail for up to $50 are sold as slightly irregulars for $21.99. Work shoes that normally retail for up to $30 are sold (again, irregulars) at $17.50. Special sales are held in April, August, and November.

Riverside Outlet. Riverside Manufacturing Co. Riverside Ave. Open Mon.–Fri. 10–4, Sat. 8–1. This outlet carries two- and three-piece men's suits by name New York manufacturers, sport coats, slacks, designer men's shirts, and sportswear. Recent savings included a New York manufacturer suit that listed for $200 marked to $89.95. Some savings are even greater during special sales held in spring and summer. Designer shirts that retail for $24 sell here from $8–$12.

- **NEWBURYPORT.** *Piel Craftsmen.* 307 High St. 617-462-7012. Open Mon.–Fri. 9–12 and 1–4, Sat. 1–4. Piel Craftsmen is a small crafts production center devoted exclusively to the production of hand-made detailed ship models. The center employs two full-time and three part-time craftsmen who may be watched at the shop as they work.

- **NORTH ATTLEBORO.** *Jewelry City Store, Inc.* Ken and Anita Porter. 4544 Kelley Blvd. (Rt. 152). 617-699-2619. Open Mon.–Sat. 10–5; Thanksgiving to Christmas: Mon.–Fri. 9–9, Sat. 9–5. This discount store carries men's belts, travel items, religious items, leather wallets, and 14-karat gold filled and sterling jewelry as well as jewelry boxes. Savings on most stock in this store range from 30–50 percent off regular list prices. Jewelry repair and machine engraving service are also available. One line that is featured at this store is Dante leather products, sunglasses, and gifts.

- **NORTH DARTMOUTH.** *Kay Windsor Outlet.* V. F. Corporation. 375 Faunce Corner Rd. (Rt. 195 E or W to exit 12—¼ mi. to outlet). 617-998-2181. Mon.–Fri. 10–9 P.M., Sat. 9:30–5. The factory outlet offers missy and half-size dresses, skirt suits, pant suits, and sportswear at discounts of 50 percent off retail prices. There are also seasonal clearance sales and special promotional sales when goods are marked down even farther.

- **PLAINVILLE**. *Le Dor Jewelry Company, Inc.* O. E. Olson. 44 Washington St. (Rt. 1). 617-695-6842. Open Mon.–Sat. 9–5; from Thanksgiving to Christmas Mon.–Fri. 9–9 and Sat. 9–5. This outlet features gold-filled, sterling silver, 14-karat gold and scrimshaw jewelry and watches. Typical savings are rings at 33 percent off list; Bulova, Caravelle, and Seiko watches at 25 percent off list prices, and Amity Leather less 33 percent.

- **PLYMOUTH**. Plymouth is a rich source of antiques and crafts shops as well as many gift and souvenir shops. Visitors who plan to stop in this historic area should write or visit the following sources of travel information (shoppers should mention the particular kinds of stores they are seeking): Plymouth County Development Council, P.O. Box 1620, Pembroke, MA 02359; and Plymouth Area Chamber of Commerce, 85 Samoset St., Plymouth, MA 02360.

Plymouth Outdoor Art Show. Brewster Gardens. Mid-Sept. The Plymouth Outdoor Art Show is quite large and features artists from southeastern Massachusetts. There are craft demonstrations and concerts in addition to the arts and crafts sale. The week-long show is held in mid-September.

For information write Plymouth Guild, Box 1000, Plymouth MA 02360.

- **REHOBOTH**. *Mendes Antiques*. Val Mendes. Rt. 44. 617-336-7381. Open year-round daily 9–6. Mr. Mendes carries antiques only, including a large selection of Early American antique furniture (eighteenth and early nineteenth century), chests, desks, tables, cupboards, clocks, and, his specialty, restored and refinished four-poster rope beds available in twin, double, queen, and king sizes. He also has beds in their original sizes bearing their original old paint. Recent offerings included a William and Mary chest, Massachusetts, 1690–1710 ($4775), a Hepplewhite four-poster canopy bed, 1780–1790 ($3500), and an American bachelor chest with beaded moulding and a wide overhanging top ($850).

- **ROCKPORT**. *Bearskin Neck*. The Bearskin Neck area consists of a small spit of land and associated breakwater that juts into the harbor at Rockport. Crammed on this narrow piece of land are dozens of old fishing shacks and small houses, most of which now contain artists' studios, craft shops, and small restaurants. Fresh seafood is also sold here. This is one of the most popular shopping spots on the north shore of Boston. Most stores are open seven days a week, especially during the high (warmer) season. Regrettably, one of the most famous sights—an old fishing shack called Motif No. 1 because of the great number of times it was painted and photographed—was lost to the relentless surf in the cruel winter of 1978.

• **SALISBURY**. *Divided House*. Larry and Mary Cuddire. 255 Elm St. (Rt. 110). 617-462-8423. Open daily 10–6. This shop offers miniatures, doll houses, dinnerware, pewter, and lamps. The doll houses are made on the premises to the owner's design. The doll houses include a Cape Cod style, five-room house with clapboards, hinged roof ($75, unpainted), and a nine-room Georgian house which opens from the front ($150). Also sold are some doll house construction material and hardware. The shop occupies the bottom five-rooms of a 250-year-old home with original fireplaces and paneling.

• **SAUGUS** (see also **Derby, CT**.). *Tiffany House Lighting Fixtures*. Augustine's Plaza (Rt. 1 north). 617-233-3601. Call for hours. Discounts on hand-crafted stained glass lighting fixtures.

• **SEEKONK**. *Leonard's Antiques, Inc*. Robert Jenkins. 600 Taunton Ave. (Rt. 44, less than 1 mi. off Rt. 114A). 617-336-8585. Open all year Mon.–Sat. 8–5 and Sun. 1–5. Leonard's handles mostly early American antique furniture. They specialize in early rope beds, restoring them to take standard bedding. Mr. Jenkins has more than three hundred beds in stock. There is also a large selection of antique furniture both in rough and restored and refinished conditions. The shop, which maintains a cabinetmaker's shop for restorations, is located in a replica of an early Cape house with spacious showroom additions. The business was established at this location in 1944.

• **SOUTHBORO**. *Willoughbrook 1680 Farm*. Framingham Rd. 617-485-1680. Open Tues.–Sat. 9–6 and Sun 10–6. Closed Mon. This wonderful old country store is a blend of the authentic old country store with some souvenir and tourist items available too. The store is housed in a beautiful, very old one-room store with wideboard floors. It is best known locally for its prime aged meats, including a wide selection of game in season. Much of the meat, including the beef and buffalo, is raised on the farm across the street. There is always a herd of these proud, plains animals on view in the field immediately adjacent to Framingham Road. The farm animals and a selection of old-fashioned country store items make this store a fun stop for all members of the family.

• **STOUGHTON**. *Twin Kee Manufacturing Company*. 720 Park St. (Rt. 27). 617-344-4751. Open Mon.–Sat. 8–6, Thurs. and Fri. evenings until 9 P.M. This is the factory outlet store for Twin Kee, manufacturers of rainwear for the entire family. The rainwear is sold at discounted prices.

• **TAUNTON**. *The Silver Shop*. Taunton Silver Manufacturers. 42 Main St. (Rt. 44). 617-823-7311. Open Mon.–Sat. 9:30–5:30, Fri. until 8:30 P.M. Taunton Silver manufactures silver plate, pewter, cutlery, jewelry, and stainless and sterling flatware. The Silver Shop sells these items at substantial discounts. The first quality pewter and silverplate is sold at 40 percent off retail prices and second quality at 55–60 percent off. The closeouts of silverplate, pewter, holloware, and jewelry are discounted by 40 percent or more.

• **WELLESLEY**. *Eastern Mountain Sports*. 189 Linden St. (Finast shopping center). 617-237-2645. Open Mon.–Fri. 9–9, Sat. 9–5:30. See **North Conway, NH** for information.

The Galleries. Norma Trust Sherman. 464 Washington St. (Rt. 128 to Rt. 16 west). 617-235-8296. Open Mon.–Sat. 10–5 or by appointment. The Galleries feature fine art (graphics, paintings, and sculpture), an intriguing collection of antique prints, contemporary jewelry, ceramics, blown glass and weaving. As a center for retail of fine arts and crafts, The Galleries have a staff of professionally trained fine artists who are art consultants to area architects and interior designers. Some of the artists and their works represented here are Stephen Fellerman's blown glass ($40), Ursala Bluestone's candleabra ($34), Marlis Schratter's large floor planter ($64), and Beatrice Achorn's ceramic mirrors ($12 to $45).

The Gifted Hand. Diane J. Reese and Glenn Johnson. 32 Church St. (3 mi. west of Rt. 128 on Rt. 16). 617-235-7171. Open Mon.–Sat. 10–5:30, in Dec. evenings and Sun. This is a contemporary crafts gallery featuring fine quality American craftsmanship. The owner is the designer and creator of Comfy Cactus © soft sculpture. Besides Comfy Cactus the gallery exhibits and sells decorative and functional pottery and porcelain, Raku, one-of-a-kind furniture, sculpture, quilts, fiber arts, stained glass, blown glass, and leather.

• **WINCHESTER**. *Golden Post Antiques*. Judith Boynton. 15 Mt. Vernon St. 617-729-3065. Open Mon.–Sat. 10–5. Ms. Boynton carries a general line of antiques and collectibles, and has a particular interest in antique stained glass. Recent offerings included a rose medallion bowl, 12 in. ($350); a pair of Bradley and Hubbard book-ends, bronze ($195); and several old clocks ($85–$350). This shop avoids depression glass, carnival glass, and bottles.

• **WOBURN**. *Abbott Arts*. Nancy Abbott Fowle. 8 Cedar St. (exit 38 off Rt. 128). 617-933-0096. Open Oct.–May, Tues.–Fri. 1:30–4:30; June–Sept. by appointment. Abbott Arts offers gift items—some handcrafted and some imported. Also sold are needlework (crewel and needlepoint) supplies. There are handcrafted toys, jewelry, pottery, weavings, and silk-screened hankies and scarves. The imports include Swedish glass, English teapots, and Scandinavian stainless steel. The handcrafts shop is located in an old nineteenth-century family homestead. Coffee is served by the old black stove in the kitchen and the rooms are devoted to needlepoint and crewel lessons and to the gifts and supplies.

CAPE COD AND THE ISLANDS

Visitors can get helpful travel information by writing the Cape Cod Chamber of Commerce, Rts. 6 and 132, Hyannis, MA 02601, 617-362-3225. If you plan an extended stay on Cape Cod you should consult the excellent regional travel guide *The Family Guide to Cape Cod* by Bernice Chesler and Evelyn Kaye (Barre

Publishing, Barre, MA. 1976), which may prove quite helpful.

• **BOURNE**. *Bournedale Country Store*. 26 Herring Pond Rd. (exit 2 off Rt. 3). 617-888-4400. Open June 1 to Oct. 1, daily 10–5. April, May, Oct., and Nov. weekends only. Closed Dec.– March. This country store is located in a 150-year-old former inn used by travelers en route to the farther reaches of the Cape. The store has a hurdy gurdy, player piano, pot-belly stove, and pickles in the barrel. Penny candy is sold from an old baggage cart from Boston's South Station. The store carries a wide selection of typical country store items and also has a barn filled with handmade gifts of many types. There are four rooms of antiques here, including furniture (oak, pine, and wicker), jewelry, china (hand-painted and Oriental porcelain), paper, advertising, toys, doll houses, tools, copper, sterling silver, posters, paintings, clocks, miniatures, and books.

• **BREWSTER**. *Brewster Pottery*. Marion Eckhardt. 437 Harwich Rd. 617-896-3587. Open in summer daily 9–6 and off season on weekends. Marion Eckhardt operates her crafts shop in a rustic, original Cape Cod house where she carries her own wheel-thrown, slab and coil pottery and batiks. Her work includes large salad bowls ($45), bird baths ($50), tea pots ($25), and batiks ($350). A complete line of pottery is available.

• **BUZZARDS BAY**. *Antique Mart*. James B. Potts, Jr. 61 Main St. (across from the RR Station). 617-759-9902. Open year-round Sat.–Mon. 9–5; summers every day except Tues. and Wed. 9–5. The Art Mart contains fifteen antique dealers under one roof. They are located on the third floor of the old Hotel Buzzards Bay, overlooking the Cape Cod canal and the famous railroad bridge. With so many dealers, there is bound to be an antique or collectible for every taste. There are lamps and parts, Hummels and china, cut and Sandwich glass, dolls and accessories, furniture, jewelry, and much more.

• **CHATHAM**. *Chatham Festival of the Arts*. Chase Park. August. This juried show has been held since 1972 under the sponsorship of the Creative Arts Center of Chatham, Box 368, Chatham, MA 02633, 617-945-9821.

Odell's. Tom and Carol Odell. 423 Main St. (½ mi. east of

Rotary). 617-945-3239. Open in summer 10–5, closed Sun.; spring and fall, Thurs.–Sat. 10–5; Jan.–Mar. by appointment. The Odells feature original design gold and silver jewelry by Tom and hand-screened fabrics by Carol. The silver earrings range from $8–$40, silver necklaces from $25–$200, and the gold jewelry from $20–$500. Carol's fabrics sell for $8–$12 a yard and she has tote bags for $14.50. The fabric is sometimes on sale September to December. The shop is located in a beautiful nineteenth-century Greek Revival sea captain's house in Old Chatham.

● **DENNIS PORT**. *Handscapes*. Diane L. Thibault and Leo C. Thibault. 148 Main St. (Rt. 28). 617-394-6657. Mid-March–June 30, 10–6; July–Aug., 10–10; Sept.–Oct., 10–9; Nov.–Dec., 10–6. The shop and gallery exhibit and sell handcraft items by American craftspeople. Over 100 crafts artists from fifteen states are represented here, many from New England and of course some from the Cape itself. There is an enormous assortment and range of crafts and prices here; toys in many media and jewelry of all kinds and prices—wampum jewelry by a Cape Cod craftsman ranges from $4.50–$11. Visitors can find sale items (usually last year's crafts) from July to mid-September.

● **EAST DENNIS**. *Eden—Hand Arts*. Eve and John Carey. Rt. 6A and Dr. Lord's Rd. (1 mi. beyond Cape Playhouse in Dennis). 617-385-9708. Open summers only, Mon.–Sat. 10–5. The Careys sell only objects they themselves make, often with the help of their children. Eve specializes in high temperature, wheel-thrown, majolica decorated functional pottery, unique in the U.S. John makes gold and silver jewelry, sculptural stained glass, and weathervanes to order. The shop is located in a small, unusual, building in a secluded tiny garden next to the Careys' half Cape house which is over 150 years old.

● **HYANNIS**. *Annual Antiques Fair*. National Guard Armory. South St. Mid-July. This fair usually runs for four days. For information contact the Chamber of Commerce (Junction of Rts. 6 and 132) or call 617-362-3225. The Hyannis Board of Trade also has an information booth at 319 Barnstable Rd. (617-775-2201).

Antique Fair. National Guard Armory. This antique fair is held in mid-July and is a five-day event, Friday–Monday, 2–10

P.M. and Tuesday, 12–5 P.M. Call 617-362-3225 for information.

Kittery Mills. 585 Main St. (Rt. 132 to Main St., west end). 617-775-6122. Open 10 A.M.–10 P.M. Mon.–Sat., spring, fall, and winter; daily in summer. The Kittery Mills offer top quality brands and designer brands ladies clothing (sportswear and dress) at discounts of 50 percent off retail. They carry Christian Dior, Givenchy, Diane Von Furstenberg, Jones N.Y., and many more.

● **NORTH EASTHAM**. *The Glass Eye.* John Knight. Eastham Village Green. 617-255-5044. Open July–Dec. daily 9–5, Jan.–June Mon.–Sat. 9–5. This shop offers functional and decorative glasswork, custom glasswork, and functional and decorative pottery. Also included are stained glass windows, panels, lamps, planters, ornaments, craft supplies, jewelry, beads, enamels, and photography.

Serendipity. Ed and Kay Deegan. Massasoit Rd. (off Rt. 6). 617-255-3274. Open 10–5 May–Dec. Other times by chance or appointment. Serendipity specializes in showing the work of these two craftspeople. Ed's specialty is one-of-a-kind rings in 14-karat and 18-karat gold using a variety of gems and gemstones. Kay produces Oshibana, the Japanese art of flower collage as well as collographs and woodcuts. The shop is located in an eighteenth-century barn off the highway. In the winters when the barn is closed due to lack of heat, the visitors are welcome to Ed's studio in their bow-roofed three-quarter Cape house, which dates back to about 1750.

● **ORLEANS**. *Cape Cod Antiques Exposition.* Nauset Regional Middle School. First weekend of August. The Information Booth on Rt. 6 (617-255-1386) should be able to provide exact dates and times if you call in the summer months.

Society of Cape Cod Craftsmen, Inc. Nauset Middle School. Early August (rain or shine). This three-day crafts fair is held under the "Big Top," and attracts thousands of visitors every year. In this show, the Society of Cape Cod Craftsmen, a juried group of artists, presents a wide variety of crafts including weavings, cabinet-making, silk screened prints and cards, carved birds, macrame, lapidary, pewter, ship models, toys, doll houses, Polish paper cutting and Easter eggs, leather crafts, flower collages, metal crafts, stained glass, woodcrafts, carvings, scrimshaw, enamels, patchwork, bronze, Sandwich glass jewelry, and spinning.

● **PROVINCETOWN**. *Remembrances of Things Past*. Helene Lyons. 376 Commercial St. (corner of Pearl St.). 617-487-9443. Open 10 A.M.–11 P.M. early spring to Jan. 1 and other times by appointment. Helene Lyons specializes in stained glass, turn-of-the-century American antiques, old advertising, and old jewelry. The shop is in a building once occupied by Captain John Cook who led an arctic expedition. Eugene O'Neill wrote about the captain's wife, Viola, in a one-act play, *Ile*.

● **SAGAMORE**. *Pairpoint Glass Works*. 851 Sandwich Rd. (Rt. 6A, under the Sagamore Bridge on the Cape side). 617-888-2344. Factory Store open daily 8–6:30; glass blowing, Mon.–Fri. 8–4:30, except holidays. The Pairpoint Glass Works produces hand-made lead crystal, and engraves, cuts, and decorates it here. The Factory Store sells the first quality glass and also carries seconds, over-runs, design samples and experimental pieces.

The Pairpoint and Mount Washington Glass factories merged and operated out of New Bedford for seventy-five years and are best known for the formulas for tinted Burmese and Peachblow glasses and the rare Mount Washington Rose paperweight.

● **SOUTH YARMOUTH**. *Woodcraft*. Tom Frazier. Old Town House Rd. 617-394-5293. Open year round Mon.–Sat. 10–6. Woodcraft exhibits and sells handcrafted wood furniture and wood accessories such as cutting boards and serving pieces. Wooden toys are priced from $1 and up. The pine furniture ranges from $50–$350. Two of the woodcraft exhibitors are Albert Kaufman and John McLeod. At the end of summer the shop holds a clearance sale.

● **WAREHAM**. *Roadside Antiques*. William B. Canedy. 3247 Cranberry Hey (Rts. 6 and 28). 617-759-7935. Open year-round daily 10–5. Mr. Canedy's special interest is in brass beds of which he always has an extensive selection. His shop also has kerosene lamps, panel lamps, nautical items, fireplace equipment, and selected pieces of furniture. Recent offerings included an iron and brass double bed ($700), an 1875 pull-down kerosene lamp with original font, shade and smoke bell ($350) and a signed Sail Bros.

panel lamp ($275). He specifically avoids bottles and books.

Tremont Nail Company. 23 Elm St. (off Rt. 28). 617-295-0038. Open June–Dec. daily 10–5, Jan.–May Tues.–Sat. 10–5, Sun. 12–5. Closed Mon. The Tremont Nail Company was founded in 1819 and has been making nails since. The main factory building was built in 1848 by ship carpenters who hand-pegged the massive timbers together. Today, the mill continues the tradition of nail making and sells a variety of old-fashioned nails that are useful for house restoration projects and "antique" decorations. These nails are sold in their old Company Store, a one-room outbuilding which once served as the general store for the mill families. Also in this building is a collection of candles, soaps, spices, teas, fresh ground peanut butter, cheese, bacon, doll house miniatures, assorted barrels (the same old fashioned barrels still used by Tremont Nail for their products) and a wide range of reproduction antique hardware products. In addition to these smaller gifts, the shop carries several top lines of high-efficiency wood burning stoves.

● **WELLFLEET**. *Connoisseur Shop.* Leonard Polak. East Main St. 617-349-2854. Open daily May–Nov. 10–5. This shop specializes in European and Oriental antiques and old prints and paintings. Specialties include Oriental porcelains, netsukes, Japanese woodblock prints, and snuff bottles. This shop does not carry any Americana.

● **WEST CHATHAM**. *Roger Harvey, Silversmith–Goldsmith.* 1409 Main St. (Rt. 28, south side). 617-945-1444. Memorial Day–Labor Day, Mon.–Sat. 10–6 or by appointment. Roger Harvey designs and makes jewelry using a variety of techniques and metals, and the prices range from $15 to $300. Chatham Historical Society has researched the house where the shop is located and found it to be over 300 years old.

● **WEST FALMOUTH**. *Saconesset Homestead Flea Market.* Rt. 28A. Every Sunday, late May to mid-Oct., 10–6. This popular flea market operates all summer on Sundays only and is fun for browsing and buying. A small parking fee (25¢) is charged for each car.

● **WEST YARMOUTH**. *Flea Market. West Yarmouth Congregational Church.* Rt. 28. Mid-June 10–4. The Flea Market features odds and ends, treasures from the attic, children's table and baked goods, and cheeses. For dates call the West Yarmouth Chamber of Commerce, 617-775-4133.

Martha's Vineyard

• **EDGARTOWN**. *The Handworks*. John and Claudia Bradford. Winter St. 617-693-9215. Open mid-May to mid-Sept. Mon.–Sat. 10–10, Sun 11–2; mid-Sept. to mid-May open weekends only. The Bradfords' shop carries a line of handcrafts, contemporary furniture, dinnerware, and cards. The handcrafts include functional pottery, weaving, bone jewelry, lithographs, toys, and silver jewelry.

The Hatchdoor. Barry Simm. Upper Main St. 617-627-4050. Open May–Oct. daily 10–10. This combination antique and crafts shop sells functional handwork from all over the world and hatchcover furniture. Among their special offerings are gold jewelry, baskets (of unusual types only), antique textiles from Central and South America, wicker, decorator lamps, leather and canvas bags, functional pottery, and clothing. The cloth is hand-woven in Guatemala to their specifications and clothing is made from their patterns.

• **OAK BLUFFS**. *Ayn's Shuttle Shop*. Ayn Chase. Lake Ave. (on the Harbor front). 617-693-0134. Open mid-June–mid-Oct. daily 9–9. The Shuttle Shop offers all handcrafted items. Ayn's specialities include weaving, lampshades, batik, basketry, and macrame. She also carries craftwork of local artists in varied media—enameling, etched glass, knitting, jewelry of all sorts, small paintings, pottery, calico items, wooden toys, and stuffed animals. The various craftspeople and their arts are featured once a week in local ads with a special display in the shop window. The shop is located in a Victorian style hotel (Wesley House) built in 1892 which still has the original lobby. The shop is not far from the famous Gingerbread Cottages of the Methodist Campground.

Martha's Vineyard Craftsmen Fair. Wesley House Hotel. 617-693-0134. July. This fair is sponsored by Martha's Vineyard

Craftsmen (Box 1207, Oak Bluffs, MA 02557) and is currently in its tenth year of offering the crafts of Massachusetts craftspeople.

• **VINEYARD HAVEN**. *Travis Tuck Studio*. Art Worker's Guild. State Rd. 617-693-3914. Open Mon.–Sat. 10–6. Mr. Tuck's studio features his very special sculpture and custom metalwork. Most of his work is done on a commission basis, but some of his lamps and weathervane designs are always on display. His usual media are hollow copper repoussé and hand-forged iron, and his work includes fountains, gates and railings, custom architectural projects, as well as the lamps and weathervanes mentioned above. One recent project was a series of street lamp reproductions for a local park. The copper street lamp (32 in. high) with hand-blown bullseye lens is $280. A Striped Bass weathervane (one of the finest metal weathervanes we have seen) 30 in. long made of hollow copper repoussé is $750. A Canada Goose weathervane of the same construction with a 44 in. wingspan is $1,500.

Nantucket Island

Nantucket has many antique shops and arts and crafts galleries. The majority of these are found in Nantucket town, where nautical and whaling antiques and crafts are in abundance. Visitors to the island should be sure to see the famous Nantucket Lightship Baskets, which have been made here since the mid-1800s by men stationed on the lightships guarding the shoals. The baskets are still made and sold on the island today. Visitors interested either in antiques or crafts may ask shopkeepers for lists or recommendations, or contact the Nantucket Chamber of Commerce for a booklet listing shops and other businesses. A list of antique dealers containing a map of the town and the phones and addresses of some twenty dealers is also available from the Chamber of Commerce, 617-228-1700.

Rhode Island

As our smallest state, Rhode Island has the fewest shops and fairs. However, Rhode Island has remained more off the beaten track in recent years, and therefore shoppers will find that it offers fine, uncrowded, leisurely shopping and merchandise of the highest quality. Because this state is smaller than its neighbors, we have listed the shops on a statewide basis, alphabetically by town.

Before leaving on your trip to see Rhode Island, we recommend that you send for two free and very helpful booklets entitled *This is Rhode Island* and *Guide to Rhode Island* both of which are filled with travel suggestions and lists of seasonal events. Also ask for the State Department of Transportation road map. To obtain these, write to the Rhode Island Department of Economic Development, Tourist Promotion Division, Weybosset Hill, Providence, RI 02903, or call 401-277-2601.

- **BRISTOL.** *Annual Harvest Fair.* Coggeshall Farm. Colt State Park. Mid-Sept., daily 1–5. This annual event features carriage rides, johnnycake, haystack sliding and crafts demonstrations.

Chamber Pot Antiques and Alfred's. Alfred Brazil, Jr. 297, 331, 327 Hope St. 401-253-3465 Open the year round daily from 10 A.M to 5 P.M. Alfred's shop was built in 1807 and is next to a beautiful house with four carved eagles from a clipper ship. Chamber Pot sells a wide range of antiques and gifts and has many collectibles. Alfred has been running this shop since he was eighteen years old.

- **CAROLINA.** *James E. Scudder.* Rt. 112 (exit 3E, I-95 north to Rt. 138 to Rt. 112). 401-364-7228. Open all year, Tues.–

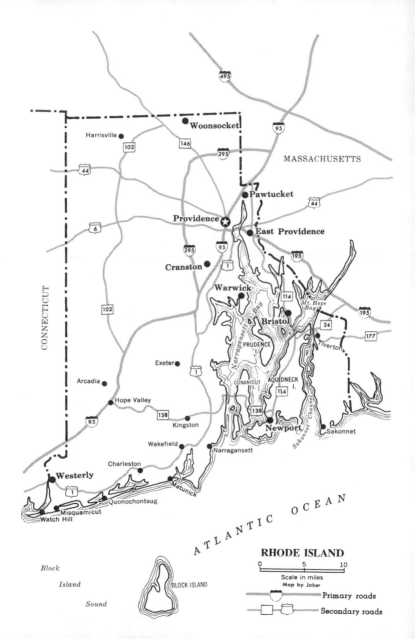

Woonsocket

Harrisville •

MASSACHUSETTS

CONNECTICUT

Pawtucket

Providence

East Providence

Cranston

Warwick

Bristol

Mt. Hope Bay

PRUDENCE I.

Narragansett Bay

Exeter •

Arcadia •

CONANICUT I.

AQUIDNECK I.

Tiverton

Hope Valley

Kingston

Newport

Sakonnet

Wakefield

Narragansett

Sakonnet Channel

Charleston

Westerly

Matunick

Quonochontaug

Misquamicut

Watch Hill

ATLANTIC OCEAN

RHODE ISLAND

0   5   10

Scale in miles
Map by Jaber

Block

Island

Sound

BLOCK ISLAND

Primary roads

Secondary roads

Sat. 10–5. Mr. Scudder's shop is well known in Rhode Island. He carries an excellent line of better quality antiques and a few currently desirable collectibles. There is Early American furniture in maple, pine, cherry, and mahogany. Most of the furniture is ready to use, some is in the rough. The shop also has early fine glass, china, and a variety of interesting items.

• **CHARLESTOWN**. *The Fantastic Umbrella Factory, Inc.* Robert Bankel. Old Post Rd. (off Rt. 1 on scenic 1A next to the Naval Air Station). 401-364-6616. Open year-round 10–5, Jan.–Feb. on weekends only. In the off-season the days vary so call first. The Fantastic Umbrella Factory, now in its tenth year, was once a working farm. The main house and wonderful old barn were built around 1790. The front store (1880) served as the meeting hall for Narragansett Temple of Honor, a temperance group. The cow shed attached to the old barn now houses a restaurant, which features johnnycake, crepes, seafood dinners, and vegetarian dishes, as well as desserts and breads baked in their kitchen. There are gardens and a full variety of farm animals strolling about. The farm complex is grouped around the central flower garden and includes the Long Shed which houses two stores—a toy and game store with hand-crafted wooden toys, fancy coloring books and an array of kites and puzzles; and a clothing boutique featuring antique clothes and feather jewelry. Next is the Front Store—a crafts building featuring pottery, leather, brasswork, weavings, and jewelry (original designs in silver and gold with precious stones). The Main Barn houses a broad scope of unusual items in various nooks and crannies of this enormous, hand-hewn structure. Here you will find records (predominantly classical, bluegrass, and dulcimers) and hand-blown glass. Upstairs in a loft is an antique store featuring unusual and federal and empire vintage (1810–1845) antiques, and many functional and unusual items (jams and preserves, Central American ware, jewelry and pottery from around the world). It is definitely a wonderful place to spend a few hours!

Amy Starrett Antiques. Tockwotten Cove. (1 mi. south off Rt. 1). 401-364-6806. Open daily May 1–Oct 15 10–5. Amy Starrett specializes in antique glass, china, copper, and brass. She carries some furniture. The shop is simply charming as is its owner and is well worth the trip down the winding little beach road to the beautiful gray shingled home overlooking the beach and salt pond.

Windswept Farm Antiques. Rt. 1 (Burlingame State Park exit). 401-364-3333. Open off season Wed.–Sun. 10–6; summer hours were not finalized at publication but are expected to be Tues.–Sun. 10–6 and evenings. Windswept Farms is a collection of interesting shops and a pub and restaurant housed in the beautiful old stone barns of a colonial farm. The Antiques Fair is in the largest barn and features a permanent collection of independent dealers in a sort of antique mall which utilizes the hand-hewn old stalls and lofts. There is a gift shop and an old Pub (open all day and evenings); on Memorial Day weekend the restaurant will be open serving authentic colonial fare. The Farm also has plans for opening a theater.

● **CRANSTON.** *Barb's Antiques and Plants.* Barbara L. Gornstein. 1982 Broad St. (off Rt. 95). 401-467-5930. Tues.–Sat. 11–5. The shop is located in historic Pawtuxet Village and specializes in eighteenth- and nineteenth-century Victorian furniture and wicker. It also carries glass, china, linens, and 1880–1900 clothes and furs. Barb's carried a Raccoon coat ($100) and a round oak table with four press back chairs ($350).

Lillian's Antiques. Lillian S. Anderson. 718 Reservoir Ave. (Rt. 2) 401-943-0554. Open all year Wed.–Sat. 12–5; open Sun. in Dec. Lillian's slogan is "the old, the odd, the beautiful." She carries a very extensive and varied collection of general antiques. There recently were wicker chairs ($35–$95), wicker couches ($125–$200) and an oak Larkin Desk in mint condition ($125).

Magi Deco to Dynasty Antiques. Margaret Motola. 2166 Broad St. (Pawtuxet Village). 401-781-6222. Open all year Mon., Wed., Fri. and Sat. 11–5. Magi features all phases of Art Deco: furniture, jewelry, and fabrics. Recently the shop had a Lalique "Little Sparrows" bowl, signed ($175), and a Tiffany iridescent candle lamp shade, signed "L C T" ($225). The shop is in the historic area on the waterfront where the Gaspee Days festival is held in summer.

● **EAST GREENWICH.** *Which Craft Studio.* Marion Deekle. 11 Division St. (north end of town, behind the Exxon station). 401-885-1526. Open all year, 10–5, closed Mon. Classes are held during the day. Which Craft Studio exhibits and sells the handcrafts of area artists. The Studio also houses several classrooms upstairs for the study of a variety of crafts such as totichomania (decoupage under glass), quilling (a single session class), macrame, dip and drape, Tole, decoupage, and eggshell crafts (taught by Marion's son, Larry). The shop sells the decorated eggs, ranging in size from ostrich to tiny quail eggs. Larry Deekle makes wonderful quail egg pendants ($18–$25); Marion Deekle makes totichomania lamp bases ($150–$200). The kits for this craft cost $25–$55. The studio sells craft supplies in a variety of media including all supplies needed for the classes. They also have doll house minia-tures, scale model replicas of Williamsburg furniture, and acces-sories. Which Craft Studios is located in a nineteenth-century blue house with white trim.

• **EXETER** *(known locally as Arcadia Village). Dovecrest In-dian Trading Post.* Ferris and Eleanor Dove. Summit Rd. off Rt. 165 (next to Arcadia State Park). 401-539-7795. Open every day of the year except Christmas, 11:30–9. The Dovecrest Trading Post is run by the Doves, descendants of the famous Narragansett Tribe. The shop features Indian hand-made articles, including moccasins from many tribes, jewelry, Indian clothing and many Indian souvenirs that children will love (head dresses, bands, and beaded rings). The shop is next door to the Dovecrest Restaurant, also run by the Doves, which features authentic American Indian dishes as well as traditional restaurant fare. The hours are the same as those of the shop. During the summer, the restaurant offers traditional Indian clambakes—call for information and reservations, which are a must.

• **FOSTER CENTER.** *Welcome Rood Studio.* Elizabeth Zimmerman. South Killingly Rd. (Rt. 94). 401-397-3045. Open Thurs.–Sun. 1–5, call first in summer. This is primarily a sales out-let for functional stoneware made on the premises. Work by other craftspeople includes weaving, wall hangings, yardage, pillows, and ponchos, as well as drawings, blown glass, and forged iron. Din-nerware plates are $10, bowls $4.50, and mugs $4. The studio also carries wool for weavers. The shop is in the original general store of the Welcome Rood Tavern, dating from the 1790s. It is on the list that is known as the National Register of Historic Sites.

• **KINGSTON**. *Earthworks*. South County Art Association. Kingston Rd. 401-783-2195. This annual show features Rhode Islanders who work in clay. It is held in late spring (May or June) and the works submitted are screened by a jury.

The Fayerweather Craft Center. Eleanor H. Sickler. Rt. 138 at Rt. 108. 401-789-9072. May 1 to Jan. 1, Tues.–Sat. 11–4. The Craft Center's program of workshops, demonstrations of handicrafts and sales takes place in the historic Fayerweather Home; the Fayerweathers were one of the area's leading Indian–African families. Besides the crafts on display, visitors can see the old restored rooms of this 1820 house. The center demonstrates various handicrafts on Tuesdays at 10 A.M. in July and August. Many different crafts are sold here, among them quilts, etched pewter, leather, metalwork, and macrame. For children, there are quilted pillows with cats, bunnies, and the like, and pillows featuring Noah's Ark and Old MacDonald's Farm.

• **MANVILLE**. *Lucky Star Antiques*. Linda L'etoile. 52 Spring St. 401-769-1656. Open all year Wed.–Fri. 12–5. The shop sells all sorts of antiques from "funky junk to formal furniture." They have good quality oak and walnut furniture and specialize in decorator items such as walnut fireplace mantels and a carousel hobby horse, German, c. 1893 ($1,500). There also is a great deal of glassware (depression, Art glass, and China).

• **NEWPORT**. Newport has dozens and dozens of antique shops and craft galleries scattered throughout town and the surrounding area. Visitors will find many shops on Franklin, Thames, and Spring streets on Newport's "historic hill." Bowen's Wharf has several craft shops. The Visitor's Center at 10 America's Cup Avenue will be glad to be of assistance. For its lists and brochures, phone 401-847-1600.

Antique Dolls and Other Things. Candida Edward. 304 Thames St. (2nd floor). Shop: 401-847-8111; home: 401-847-1665. Open 10–4 by chance or appointment. The shop carries a variety of antiques and a collection of dolls for beginners and advanced collectors. Recently Ms. Edward had a French Clown made in 1890 ($275), a 16-inch Frozen Charlie ($200) and a 16-inch closed mouth

Tete Jumeau ($950). The Thames Street area of Newport contains about thirty antique shops in a small district.

Betsy's of Newport—Glitter from the Past. Betsy Kennedy and Lee Reeve. 221 Spring St. (near the post office). 401-846-7338. Open year-round by chance, 2–5. Betsy deals in vintage vogues and accessories for men and women with a few antiques and collectibles. The vintage vogues (dating from late 1800s to 1940s) are selected furs, Deco items, costume jewelry, spectacular designer clothes, elegant lingerie, and white Victorian petticoats. Betsy recently had a red organdie strapless ball gown with ostrich-feather trim and stole; and a 1930s double-breasted three-piece men's suit with large lapels and pleated, pegged trousers.

Cooper and French Gallery of Fine American Crafts. 130 Thames St. 401-849-6512. Open summer Mon.–Sat. 10–6, Sun. 1–5, and evenings on weekends; winter daily 10–5. The Cooper and French Gallery, Rhode Island's foremost craft center, represents and exhibits the leading crafts artists in the country. The gallery specializes in consulting and advising craft collectors and commissioning works in clay, glass, and fiber. The gallery houses two floors of excellent crafts in several media; in addition there are many special shows and exhibits throughout the year.

Four Ninety Two Thames Street. Joan Taylor Westman. 492 Thames St. (lower Thames St. area). 401-847-3091. Open Mar.– Dec., Mon.–Sat. 11–5. The shop offers antiques, collectibles, and special handcrafts. The crafts are made from oriental rug fragments. Joan Westman specializes in glassware, textiles, and unusual collectibles—"antiques of the bizarre." She recently had a French Empire dressing table ($350) and carries a selection of oriental rugs ($150 or less).

Harvinidge. Vincent and Marjorie Smith. 76 Spring St. (in the center of town). 401-849-2076. Open May–Sept. Mon.–Sat. 11–5:30. This shop specializes in antique pottery and porcelain, as well as in British historical items in all media—ceramics, glass, silver, textile, tin, books, etc. Harvinidge recently had a Duke of Wellington Toby Jug ($325), a George III jubilee Delft bowl ($675) and a limited edition crystal tankard—Edward VIII, 1937 ($125).

Hyde House Antiques. Paul W. Holbrook. 87 Spring St. (1

block south of town square). 401-847-7788. Open 10–5 daily except Sun. in summer; winter on weekends only. Hyde House specializes in rare books with fine bindings and interesting titles. The shop also carries a line of antique glass and collectibles. Some recent finds here were an Early History of Rhode Island ($25) and a colored engraving of a seaport ($15). The shop is located in a nineteenth-century restored townhouse on Newport's "Historic Hill."

Lamplighter Antiques. Al Lozito. 42 Spring St. 401-849-4179. Open Mon.–Sat. 12–5. The shop specializes in oil lamps, clocks, and Currier and Ives prints. It also carries a general line of antique furniture. Recently a Seth Thomas schoolhouse clock in an oak case was available ($250) as were 19-in. Brass "Ball Top" Andirons ($375).

McDonough and Larner. John Larner. 26 Franklin St. 401-849-2680. Open Tues.–Sat. 12–5; appointments advisable. The shop specializes in fine leaded glass, antique rugs, and oriental bronze, ivory, and porcelain. Mr. Larner recently had a Japanese-style leaded dogwood-tree window (3′ × 9′) for $950 and a 9′6″ × 12′6″ antique Kerman rug for $1,200.

Old Colony Shop. Marian Curran. 517 Thames St. Shop: 401-846-4918; Home: 401-847-4509. Open year-round weekdays 12–4 and by appointment. The Old Colony is an old-fashioned antique shop with a great variety of items—a little bit of everything. Ms. Curran has Victorian and coin silver, copper items, china, porcelains, and some Oriental items.

Alice Simpson Antiques. 24 Franklin St. 401-849-4252. Open year round Monday through Saturday 12–5. Ms. Simpson carries antique silver, jewelry, porcelain, and a general line of furniture. A recent find in the shop was a Haviland Tea Set with several odd pieces ($140) and a Tiffany-type shade with caramel glass ($150).

● **PAWTUCKET**. *Colonial Braided Rug Company*. 560 Mineral Spring Ave. (Rt. 15, off Rt. 122). Open Mon.–Sat. 10–5. Colonial manufactures flat and tubular braided rugs and chair pads. The Mill Outlet Store sells these products at 20–40 percent off retail prices. The Rug Company is an old nineteenth-century Rhode Island Mill in Pawtucket, on the site of Slater's Mill, America's first mill to be engaged in the manufacture of textiles.

Sweater Warehouse. 212 Dartmouth St. (behind Industrial National Bank). 401-725-5770. Open Mon.–Wed. 9–3, Thurs.–Fri. 9–9, Sat. 9–5. The Warehouse sells a selection of men's and women's sweaters at discount rates.

Weaver's Guild of Rhode Island. Annual Show and Sale. Slater's Mill. 401-725-8638. The Weaver's Guild sponsors this show annually in December at the historic site of America's first textile mill.

● **PROVIDENCE.** *Bedspread Mill Outlet.* Matthew Frauwirth. 39 Kennedy Plaza. 401-861-9536. Open Mon.–Sat. 9–5. This mill outlet sells first quality bedspreads, draperies, comforters, and blankets at 50–60 percent below retail (some savings are on closeouts). Brands carried include Bates, Normandie Bedspreads, Springmaid, Everwear, and others. Special sales held periodically feature unusual buys on some firsts, closeouts, and selected seconds at even greater savings.

● **RIVERSIDE.** *Do-Flicker Antiques.* Edmund Oliver, Jr. 884 Willett Ave. 401-433-2667. Open afternoons daily. Mr. Oliver carries antiques, collectibles, and memorabilia, and specializes in old lamps, furniture and the unusual. He recently had in his shop a lovely miniature cranberry lamp ($145), a 16-in. Mandarin Rose Medallion punch bowl ($120) and a Queen Anne Country Arm Chair, c. 1730 ($475).

● **USQUEPAUGH.** *Kenyon's Grist Mill.* Paul E. T. Drumm, Jr. Glen Rock Rd. (5 mi. east of I-95 on Rt. 138). 401-783-4054. Open July–Sept. Mon.–Fri. 1–4; Mar.–Dec. 24, weekends 12–5. Visitors can follow the milling process from grain to package at this nineteenth-century grist mill. The Grist Mill Store is across the street and sells the stone-ground products as well as cookware and New England foods. Kenyon's famous stone-ground corn meal is the main ingredient in RI Johnny Cakes; Usquepaugh sponsors a Johnny Cake Festival in October with johnnycakes and clam cakes, a craft show, and booths.

Wood and Wax Works. Yvette Nachmias Saglio. Glen Rock Rd. off Rt. 138. 401-789-0039. Open 9–6—July, Aug., Nov., Dec. Mon.–Sat.; other months weekends only. The Works sells hand-made hardwood slab tables and bread boards and unique candles which are crafted on the premises. The tables range in price from $50–$175, bread boards $7–$25 and candles from $.50 to $12 for an extravaganza. The shop also sells pottery and antiques. It is housed in a 1739 building in an old mill village by a lovely waterfall and pond.

● **WAKEFIELD**. *Annual South County Heritage Festival*. Rt. 1 (Marina Park). This week-long observance includes participating residents dressed in colorful Colonial garb, a tremendous parade, and dozens of booths, rides, crafts sales, and demonstrations. The Festival and Colonial week are held in early July.

Dove and Distaff Antiques. Caleb Davis. 472 Main St. 401-783-5714. Open daily except Sun. 8–5. This shop specializes in early American furniture and accessories. It is well known for the high quality of its antiques, also the restoring and refinishing of antiques.

● **WARWICK**. *Rocky Hill School Antique Show and Sale*. Rocky Hill School. Ives Rd. This annual antique show is held in late February. For exact dates call the Tourist Promotion Division, 401-277-2601.

● **WEST KINGSTON**. *Peter Pots Authentic Americana*. Oliver W. Greene III. Off Rt. 138. 401-783-2350. Open all year Tues.–Sat. 9–5; Sun. 1–5. Peter Pots specializes in early furniture and ceramics. The shop is located in a lovely setting; contemporary stoneware is made and sold here in a picturesque old mill. There is a branch store at 2980 Post Road, Warwick, RI (401-737-9033).

● **WOONSOCKET**. *Stitchers Inc. Retail Remnant Room*. Dan Sadwin. 1081 Social St. (jct. Rts. 114 and 126). 401-767-1500. Open Mon.–Fri. 8–3:30, Sat. 8–12 noon. Stitchers sells Cape Cod curtains, tier and panel curtains, remnants for artists and craftspeople, patchwork squares, trims, and much more at greatly reduced prices. The management is very knowledgeable, having been in the business for forty-five years, and is glad to be of assistance.

● **WYOMING**. *Meadowbrook Herb Garden*. Heinz Grotzke. Rt. 138. (1 mi. east of I-95 exit 3). 401-539-7603. Open Mon.–Fri. 10–12, 1–5; Sat. 10–12, 1–4; Sun. 1–4. Meadowbrook has a wonderful greenhouse filled with herbs of all sorts, including many unusual ones. The shop features plants, herb seasonings, and herb teas all grown on the property by means of biodynamic methods. It also sells seeds, gardening books, and handcrafted wooden toys and gifts. The gardens are fabulous in summer.

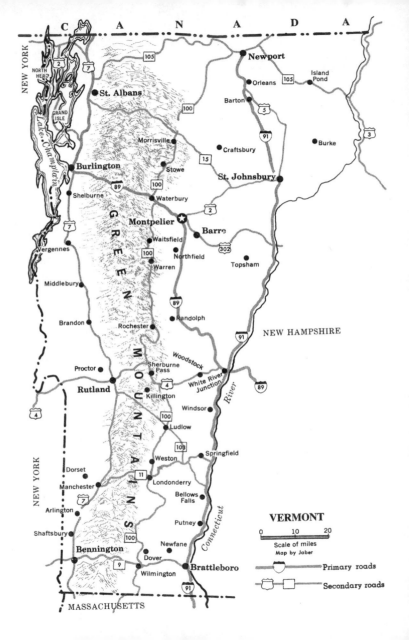

VERMONT

Scale of miles

Map by Jaber

0   10   20

Primary roads

Secondary roads

Vermont

MANY OF VERMONT'S arts-and-crafts fairs as well as antique fairs, music festivals, church suppers, and other events of interest to tourists are listed in one of three events calendars published by the State of Vermont. The calendars are seasonal, published for winter–spring, summer, and autumn events, and are available from The Vermont Travel Division, Agency of Development and Community Affairs, Montpelier, VT 05602. They are yours for the asking.

The listings of shops and fairs that follow have been divided into four groups according to geographic region (southwest, southeast, northwest, and northeast). Within each region, the listings are alphabetical by town. As a rough guide for readers, the north–south division line runs from just below Brandon to just below Thetford Center. The east–west dividing line runs from a point between Whitingham and Jacksonville on the south to a point between Montgomery Center and Westfield in the north.

SOUTHWESTERN

• **BELMONT**. *Belmont Antiques*. Box 63. 802-259-2338. Open by chance or appointment. This shop carries antiques and collectibles with emphasis on primitives, glass, china, oil lamps, and country furniture of maple, cherry, and pine. The shop also carries the Woodstock Workshop line of hand-made lampshades.

The shop is situated about 1 mile off Rt. 155 or 3 miles off Rt. 103.

• **BENNINGTON**. *Bennington Christmas Crafts Fair*. Visual and Performing Arts Center. Bennington College. Last weekend in November. The Bennington Christmas Crafts Fair is a three-day event featuring the work of sixty New England craftspeople. Admission is $1 for adults, free for children.

Old Bennington Country Store. Rt. 9 West. 802-442-3482. Open year-round Mon.–Sat. 9–5, Sun. 1–5 all year. This is a very old general store that retains many of its original fittings. On sale is a wide selection of general merchandise including spices, scented soaps, tobacco, leather, and cheese. There is an old-fashioned penny candy counter, old-time food favorites, kitchen wares, and household goods.

Old Bennington Woodcrafters. Rt. 9 West. 802-442-9014. Open year-round Mon.–Sat. 9–5, Sun. 1–5. Reproductions of Early American furniture, lamps, pewter, brass, glass, iron, mirrors, pictures, and handcrafts all displayed in a restored old carriage barn.

Betty Towne Antiques. 520 South St. 802-442-9204. Open all year Mon.–Sat. 9–5. Betty carries pattern glass (clear and colored), art glass, dolls and toys, Bennington pottery and other old pottery, lamps, early furniture, clocks, quilts, brass, copper, fine china, and prints. Recent selections included a tiger maple slant-top Chippendale desk, early ladder back rocker, pair of 10-inch blue Aurene candlesticks, and an early pine dry sink.

Wagon Wheel Woolens. Paul and Connie Koninis. 229 North St. 802-442-5639. Open July–Dec., Mon.–Fri. 9:30–8:30; Sat., Sun. 9:30–5:30. This outlet handles sweaters, blankets, hats, mittens, and gloves at discount prices. Sweaters that list for $25 are $19.95 at Wagon Wheel. The shop also holds special fall and spring sales.

Yankee Notions. Rt. 9 west. 802-442-3482. Open year-round Mon.–Sat. 9–5, Sun. 1–5. Yankee Notions is a specialty shop, serving the needs of creative sewers. Housed in an authentic 1822 one-room schoolhouse, the shop has calico prints, trimmings, buttons, needlepoint canvases, embroidery kits, quilt pieces, etc.

• **CASTLETON CORNERS**. *Old Homestead Antiques*. Alma

Donchian. Rt. 4A. 802-468-2425. Open daily June 1–Nov. 1, 9–5 and by appointment. Ms. Donchian specializes in early Americana, including furniture, primitives, lamps and other lighting, Oriental rugs, glass, and china. Recent offerings included an early American school bench ($300), early student lamp ($225) and a Captain's Desk–Davenport ($450). The shop is located in a hand-hewn barn, built c. 1830.

● **DANBY**. *Red Wagon Antiques*. Anna Burdine. 4 Corners Rd. 802-293-5404. Open May 15–Oct. 12 daily 10–5, and by chance or appointment. Ms. Burdine carries a general line with specialties including silver and blue decorated stoneware (crocks, jugs, and butter churns).

● **DORSET**. *J. K. Adams Company*. Rt. 30. 802-362-2303. Open 9–5 daily all year. J. K. Adams is a manufacturer of woodware—cheese trays, cutting blocks, lazy Susans, carving platters, butcher's blocks, knife racks, and kitchen work tables. On the second floor the factory outlet store has numerous factory seconds at reduced prices.

● **EAST ARLINGTON**. *Candle Mill Village*. Old Mill Rd. (1½ mi. east of Rt. 7). 802-375-6068. Open Memorial Day to Dec. 30, Mon.–Sat. 9–5; Sun. 12–5. All other times daily 12–5. Candle Mill Village is a collection of eight craft and specialty shops contained within three buildings on the banks of a Green Mountain stream—a 200-year-old former grist mill, a two-story hay barn, and a rambling old eighteenth-century house. Among the offerings here are over 50 thousand candles, antique clocks, gourmet cookware, fudge, quilts, jewelry books, and more. Visitors may dip their own candles and watch a potter at work.

Ice Pond Farm Antiques. Mary Coyle Schafer. 802-375-6448. Open all year, daily except Sun. 9–5:30. Ms. Schafer carries American country furniture and accessories. Recent offerings included a small painted trunk ($225) and a set of graduated Canton platters ($65–$125, each). The shop is located in the granary of the farm which was built in 1792.

● **HUBBARDTON**. *Iron Horse Antiques, Inc*. John Juby and Vernon Ward, Rt. 30. 802-273-2000. Open Nov. 1–May 15, Mon.–Fri. 9:30–5:30, Sat. by appointment; May 15–Oct. 31

Mon.–Sat. 9:30–5:30. This shop specializes in antique tools, implements and utensils for all trades and crafts. It also carries an extensive line of in-print books on tools, utensils, traditional crafts, and antiques, as well as a large collection of hard-to-find books. Iron Horse is believed to be the largest volume dealer of antique tools in North America.

● **MANCHESTER** (see **Putney**) *Basketville*. Rt. 7. Open daily, year-round.

The Jelly Mill. Rt. 7. 802-362-3494. Open daily 10–6, evenings in the summer (closed Christmas, New Year's Day, Easter, and Thanksgiving). This store is a combination country store, department store, craft, and gift shop all contained under one roof of a huge renovated dairy barn (the old jelly mill of its name was destroyed by fire in 1969). Among its many offerings are numerous homemade preserves and relishes, Vermont cheese and candy and other foodstuffs, soaps, plants and pots, cookware and kitchen utensils, and contemporary American crafts including metal sculpture, handmade lamps, imported fabrics, wall hangings, music boxes, dried flowers, porcelain, glass, weaving, jewelry, pottery, and metalwork. The shop has a resident woodcarver who does custom carving and an antique shop. There also is a luncheon restaurant with picture windows overlooking the ponds and mountains.

Paraphernalia Antiques. Anne Alenick. Rt. 7. 802-362-2421. Open May 25–Nov. 1 Mon.–Sat. 10–5. Paraphernalia carries a wide line of antiques including antique jewelry, silver miniatures, Battersea boxes, orientals, drinking vessels, weathervanes, marine paintings, English and French furniture, and art glass. The owner avoids early American primitives.

Southern Vermont Craft Fair. Manchester Recreation Area. Rt. 100. Last weekend in August (Fri., Sat., Sun.). In this three-day event the work of 100 craftspeople is displayed and sold under the tents at the Manchester Recreation Center. The Center has a swimming pool, and there is entertainment. Admission is $1 for adults, children free.

● **MANCHESTER CENTER**. *Brewster Antiques*. Cecile T. Brewster. Bonnet St. 802-362-1579. Open daily. This shop specializes in antique jewelry and sterling silver as well as in very fine glass, china, and bronzes. Their recent offerings included a diamond ring with three stones, 1½-karat Platinum ($850), solid silver bowl ($2000) and a silver cup ($125). The shop is located in an 1876 Victorian home.

Enchanted Doll House. Rt. 7 (2½ mi. north of the village). 802-362-1327. Open all year Mon.–Sat. 9–5, Sun. 10–5. This shop is crammed full of dolls, baby toys, crafts, stocking stuffers, children's books, cards, posters, children's farms, zoos, castles, cars and trains, mobiles, puppets and dollhouse miniatures as well as craft supplies for building miniature homes and furnishings. Also on display is an 1890 Victorian dollhouse complete with inlaid parquet floors.

Second Best Factory Outlet. On-the-Green. 802-362-3482. Open Mon.–Sat. 10–6. This outlet features over 10 thousand sweaters and skirts at great savings.

• **MIDDLETOWN SPRINGS**. *Nimmo and Hart Antiques*. South St. 802-235-2388. Open by appointment or by chance. This shop carries a line of early American furniture, Early English oak, eighteenth-century English pottery and porcelain, glass, and selected decorative accessories including folk art, pewter, brass, copper, tin, silver, quilts, paintings, and fabrics. Recent offerings included an all-original Massachusetts maple Queen Anne flat-top highboy ($12,000) and an early nineteenth-century American trade sign with a handpainted sulky and driver ($2,500). The shop specifically avoids collectibles, limited editions, (eg. Franklin Mint), dolls, cottage furniture (heavily refinished pine, etc.). Nimmo and Hart is located in a restored eighteenth-century Cape Cod house.

Old Spa Shop, Inc. Sarah Kirkwood. Rts. 133 and 140. 802-235-2366. Open mid-May–Dec. 1, 10:30–5. Closed Mondays. The Old Spa Shop specializes in mint condition Victorian furniture including ladies' and gentlemen's chairs, carved turtleback marble top tables, Empire chests, desks, Empire sofas, Victorian occasional chairs, and fainting benches. They also have Victorian china, glassware, and girandole sets. The shop avoids Eastlake and oak. It is located in a red brick house (1814) that is listed in the Vermont Historic Registry.

- **MOUNT HOLLY**. *The Blacksmith Shop*. Pete Taggett. (between Rutland and Ludlow, off Rt. 103; write or call for directions, or ask at the post office). 802-259-2452. Open Tues.–Sat. 9–4:30. Pete Taggett limits the production of his one-man hand-forge shop to fireplace accessories including a special line designed for use with Jotul box stoves. As an example of current prices, he asks $37.50 for a four-piece Jotul accessory set with shovel, poker, hoe, and broom.

- **PERU**. *The Bromley Mountain Craft Fair*. Base Lodge, Bromley Mountain. Rt. 11. Last Weekend in September. This fair carries forty selected exhibits indoors at the base lodge. Admission is free. For exact dates and times contact Bromley Mountain at 802-824-5522.

- **POULTNEY**. *Elbow Bend II*. Ruth L. Anderson. Lake Rd. (a good dirt road—watch for signs on Rt. 30). 802-287-9192. Open by chance or by appointment. This shop has a general line with varied prices. Among the specialties are Sandwich, Flo Blue, crocks, small furniture, tin, wood, pictures, Historical Blue, and some pressed glass. Ms. Anderson avoids depression glass and oak furniture.

Old China Shop. Edith Martin. 71 Main St. 802-773-9039. Open daily all year, 10–5 (winter by chance). This is a small but well-stocked shop. It specializes in fine china with a selection of Early Staffordshire to Oriental china, including Victorian pitcher and bowl sets as well as lamps, quilts, brass, copper, silverware.

- **RAWSONVILLE**. *The Rusty Horseshoe*. Bill McMillen and David Hamman. Rt. 100 (north of Rt. 30). 802-824-3805. Open May–Nov. weekends 10–5, and by chance. This shop specializes in primitive American to European furniture and accessories, mostly ones with a unique quality about them. Recent offerings included a Queen Anne drop-leaf table, Shaker laundry basket, English Deacon's bench and a carved-out tree trunk trough. The owners avoid Victorian pieces, American glass and china, collectibles, and memorabilia. The shop is located in a nineteenth-century hand-hewn barn overlooking the ski trails of *Stratton Mountain*.

- **RUTLAND**. *Eagles Nest Antiques*. Mr. and Mrs. James Lemmo. 53 Prospect St. 802-773-2418. Open all year Sat. and Sun.

by appointment or by chance. This general shop has antiques, collectibles and memorabilia, including a large selection of fine china, glassware, dolls, cast kettles, copper, miniatures, art glass, toys, Oriental rose medallions, stoneware, pattern glass, and some furniture.

Windy Ledge Antiques. Barbara B. Chiolino. 64 North Main St. 802-775-5251. Open all year by appointment only. Ms. Chiolino specializes in textiles such as quilts and coverlets (especially hand-made) stone ware, country primitives, folk art, children's items, dolls, etc. Recent offerings included textiles ranging from $10 to $1500 and children's chairs from $10 to $75. The shop is in the owner's 1812 Federal-style home which provides a pleasant setting for the items on sale.

- **SOUTH DORSET**. *The Anglophile Antiques*. Dorothy Jones. The Old Schoolhouse. Rt. 30. 802-362-1621. Open daily except Wed. 10–5. Closed in April. Ms. Jones specializes in eighteenth- and nineteenth-century English antiques including china, Georgian silver, old brass and copper, small furniture and miniatures; also featured are china, snuffs, tea caddies, scents, and writing boxes. The shop is in a large 1800s two-room schoolhouse.

- **SOUTH LONDONDERRY**. *Hearthstone Antiques*. Barbara Trask. Hearthstone Village. 802-824-3126. Open May 1–Nov. 30, Mon.–Sat. 9–5; Dec. 1–April 30 Mon.–Sat. 10–3 or by appointment. This shop handles American country and period furniture in original paint and condition whenever possible, early tin, baskets, pottery (stoneware and redware), hanging lanterns and lamps, quilts, copper, yelloware, and spongeware. Recent offerings included a pine corner cupboard, c. 1810 with panelled doors ($975), a round Shaker friendship basket in mint condition ($55), and a set of three copper pans, dovetailed and marked Portland, Maine ($250).

- **WESTON**. *Amapola Antiques*. Dolores Bersell. Rt. 100 (north of Londonderry). 802-824-3572. Open weekends, all year, and other days by appointment. Amapola specializes in country-store and antique advertising items (signs, tins, etc.) and does a large national business in antique paper goods as well as in the works of American illustrators (Rockwell, Coles, Phillips, Leyendeker, N. C. Wyeth, and others). The shop sells old magazine covers to collectors and decorators; it does *not* carry glass, china, postcards, or furniture.

Ralf Coykendall Jr., Birdcarver. Rt. 100. The shop is open most of the time, by chance. Carving and painting are in Ralf Coykendall, Jr.'s blood. His mother was an artist and his father a decoy maker. Ralf himself is not only a birdcarver (carving everything from chickadees to geese) but an author of a book on rigging decoys and on training retrievers. His carved birds are available as wall plaques or self-standing. A small sampling of the many carvings available include a Chickadee ($14.95), Nuthatch ($17.95), Meadowlark ($35), Ruffed Grouse ($45), Woodcock ($85), and Duck Decoys (old fashioned NE style, $75–$100). Many birds are available as miniatures (one-third of life size) at a proportional reduction in price.

FHB Silver Workshop. Frances Holmes Boothby. Main St. 802-824-3866. Open daily except Sun. from mid-June to mid-Sept., 10–5:30. Ms. Holmes' shop is in a remodeled shed with barn door and wrought iron fence. The shop is the outlet for more than five hundred pieces of jewelry hand made by the owner. Her work is in sterling silver and gold, and ranges in price from $4.50 to $1,200 with the majority of pieces priced under $50. The workshop is also the outlet for twelve local craftspeople whose pottery, glass, leather, and batiks are on display.

The Handcrafts Shop. Steve and Gail Wiggett Bezore. 17 Main St. (Rt. 100, the red building next to the Country Store Restaurant). 802-824-3208. Open summers only daily 10–5. Handcrafts exhibits and sells a variety of well-made crafts in a moderate price range. The shop carries pottery, macrame, silver jewelry, enamels, crochet, and a limited supply of craft materials (no kits). The Bezores make their own silver jewelry and macrame. Silver rings sell for $12–$30, and Bezores' silver bracelets sell for $5 and up. The store also features the crafts of other regional artists (Vermont and New England). There are hand-made, hand-painted, ceramic kerosene-oil lamps ($18–$25); a silver snowflake design necklace, made in Vermont ($65); and ceramic goblets and chalices ($3.50–$10). The Bezores' shop, 180-years-old, is in their old New England "joint house." The rooms, barn and woodshed were added on more or less linearly, permitting the farmer to go through the house to get to wood or feed the livestock without going outside in the cold winters. The shop is located in part of the barn and the woodshed. In one of the other rooms, adjacent to Handcrafts, is a wonderful little bookstore, The Ploughshare. It is run by Muriel Zimmermann and specializes in spiritual, philosophical, and literary titles, as well as children's books.

The Vermont Country Store, Inc. Vrest, Mildred, and Lyman Orton. Rt. 100. Open all year Mon.–Sat. 9–6. In 1945, Vrest Orton opened the first restored old-fashioned country store in this country. At the same time he was one of two small mail-order establishments to send out a national mailing of their catalog of country-store goods available by mail. This tradition continues with their *Voice of the Mountain* catalog that is mailed to thousands each year. Mr. Orton is also an author of many books and the president of the American Association of Historic Sites Officials. He is listed in *Who's Who*. The store carries a full line of country store goods, cheeses and candies, and has a pot belly stove and a checkerboard on a barrel in case you want to take on one of the local players. The store also operates a restaurant down the block which contains a handsome Victorian bedroom museum. The Vermont Country Store is clearly the best of the vast proliferation of this sort of store. Its tremendous selection of goods is top quality and the feeling of the store is authentic rather than flea market.

Weston Bowl Mill. Rt. 100. 802-824-6219. Open Mon.–Sat. 8–5, Sun. 10–5. The Weston Bowl Mill is a bowl and other woodenware factory and outlet that attracts more than 100 thousand visitors annually to the Southern Vermont location. Visitors may watch bowls being made and select merchandise from the gift shop that includes a large selection of seconds at discount prices.

• **WILMINGTON.** *Art on the Mountain.* Haystack Mountain Base Lodge. This arts-and-crafts show is held annually for one week in mid-August for the benefit of the Deerfield Valley Health Center. The works of more than a hundred artisans are exhibited, including paintings, sculpture, photography, and many crafts.

Jaffe Studio. Ed and Sandy Jaffe. Shearer Hill Rd. 802-464-8516. Open all year by chance or appointment, usually 10–5 in summer and fall except Tues. and Wed. Ed Jaffe gained national repute as a photographer in New York City. Several years ago he closed his New York studio and has devoted himself since to the creation of contemporary wood sculpture and the sale of nineteenth-century antiques in pristine condition. Antique specialties include furniture, art glass, fireplace equipment, paintings, and cut glass from the period 1820–1900.

Klara Simpla. Frances Hollander. Main St. (Rt. 9). 802-464-5257. Open 10–6 daily except Wed. Klara Simpla offers "utile things"—functional items—in a variety of crafted media including metal, glass, clay, wood, and cloth. Some of the recent offerings included cutting boards ($8–$35), flameware pottery ($5–$50), blown glass ($25–$40), stained glass ($30–$35), and wooden ware. One of the crafts producers handled is Winchester Pottery (stoneware, flameware, and porcelain). The shop also carries books on crafts, graphics, drawing and painting supplies, and clay. The shop is located in a carriage house that is more than a hundred years old.

The Mount Snow Craft Fair. Base Lodge, Mount Snow. Rt. 100. Last weekend in July. This craft show displays and sells the work of more than seventy of New England's fine craftspeople in a three-day fair. Admission and entertainment are free. Contact Mount Snow (802-464-3333) for exact dates and times.

Mount Snow Foliage Festival of Craft. Base Lodge, Mount Snow. Rt. 100. First weekend of October. Held at the Base Lodge, this festival will have seventy exhibits of New England crafts for the three-day (Friday, Saturday, and Sunday) weekend. Admission is $1 for adults and free for children. Call Mount Snow (802-464-3333) to confirm exact dates and times.

Quaigh Design Centre. Lilias MacBean Hart. West Main St. 802-464-2780. Open June 1–Jan. 1, daily 10–6; Jan. 1–May 30, closed Tues. and Wed. This shop devotes most of its space to New England crafts and the remainder of Scottish Woolens. The crafts line includes pottery, weaving, woodwork, stained glass, jewelry, batiks, graphics, lamps and shades, all products of Northern New

England craftspeople. The woolens (mohair, lamb's wool, and cashmere) are from the owner's family business in Scotland. Crafts demonstrations (weaving and lampshade making) are given on weekends. The shop is a traditional New England clapboard building built in 1833 with exposed beams and a two-way fireplace.

SOUTHEASTERN

• **BRATTLEBORO**. *Factory Handbag Store*. Putnam Park (exit 1 off I-91). 802-254-4594. Open daily 9–9. This factory outlet sells leather goods at 10–30 percent below retail.

Hickins Mountain Mowings Farm. Black Mountain Rd. 802-254-2141. Open every day. This unusual farm, tucked in the Dummerston Hills, offers a diversity of farm and greenhouse products that include homemade foods, plants of every kind, berries, gift packages, maple pickles and relishes, other maple products, grains and beans grown on the farm, and a wide selection of farm-fresh vegetables.

L. J. Serkin Company. Lucy and John Serkin. 51 Elliot St. 802-257-7044. Open Mon.–Sat. 9:30–5:30. The Serkins carry a full line of carefully selected crafts from a great number of craftspeople whose work includes pottery, jewelry, batik, woodworking, wrought iron, blown glass, and their specialty, hand-weaving. There are two hand-weaving studios on the premises and visitors may watch work in progress. The shop also carries basic weaving and spinning supplies including imported CUM yarns from Denmark.

• **BRIDGEWATER**. *Bridgewater Mill Mall*. Rt. 4. Most stores open Mon.–Sat. 10–5, Sun. 12–5. The Bridgewater Mill was first built as a water-powered cotton mill in 1825. It was later converted into wool production and finally abandoned in the early 1970s. One man saw the historic value of the old site and convinced a group of local stockholders to form a renovation corporation to save the mill and create new jobs for the village. Several years later the restoration (including foot-wide beams and original oiled floors) was complete and the mill was designated a National Historic Site. The mill now houses a number of shops and a small restaurant. Among the shops are Bridgewater Leather Company (802-672-3671) which sells original design, hand-made leather goods. Vermont Clock Craft (802-672-3456) carries their own original design clocks, hand-made of select Vermont pine with West German movements. Brindalwood . . . A Craft Shop (802-672-5144) has a complete selection of American crafts including pottery, batik, weaving, blown glass, wooden and stuffed toys, mirrors, lamps, wood products, and jewelry. Sterling and Stones, and Fabrics and Findings (802-672-5130) are two shops run as one with jewelry (sterling, from local and U.S. sources) and fabrics including patchwork, stuffed toys, hand-woven and hand-knit items and sewing/crafts supplies.

● **CHESTER.** *Fieldfarm Antiques.* Arthur Bratton. 802-875-2454. The shop is open from 10–5 all year, when the owner is home. Mr. Bratton operates his shop in a one-and-a-half story brick cottage (1822) that was extensively changed later to the Victorian style with characteristic high gables and fancy shingles. The shop specializes in painted furniture, fabrics, tiles, paintings, mirrors, and hooked rugs.

● **GRAFTON.** *Grafton Antiques.* Mary E. Hinkle. Rt. 35. 802-843-2254. Open Thurs., Fri., Sat. 1–5, Sun. 2–5. Other times by chance or appointment. Grafton Antiques is housed in an early (c. 1860) house which was moved to the village in sections in 1909. The shop specializes in period country furniture, portraits, metal, wood objects, Chinese export, and tools.

● **HARTLAND.** *Barbara E. Mills, Antiques.* Rt. 5 (exit 9 off I-91, then north about 2 mi.). 802-436-2441. Open May–Oct. 9–9; rest of year by appointment or chance. Barbara Mills carries eighteenth- and early nineteenth-century New England antiques, primarily furniture; primitive, country, and some formal. She also carries china, glass, iron, tin, accessories, (spinning wheels, yarn winders, etc.), copper, brass, quilts, and pottery. Recently the shop offered a four-door raised panel cupboard, top molding and original blue paint ($850); and a restored four-drawer (graduated) chest in curly birch with french foot and oval Hepplewhite brasses ($550). Barbara Mills avoids Victorian, oak, and twentieth-century items. The shop is in one of Vermont's oldest brick Federal houses, built in 1804 by colonial architect Asher Benjamin. In addition to the antique shop there are accommodations for overnight guests.

- **HEALDVILLE.** *Crowley Cheese and Vermont Crafts Shop.* Randolph B. Smith. Rt. 103. 802-259-2210. Open Mon.–Sat. 10–5, Sun. 1–5. Crowley Cheese has been one of Vermont's finest for almost a century. A few years ago, when there were no descendants of the Crowley family to run the business, Mr. Smith, a retired school teacher, bought the operation. He now continues a tradition of cheese making that involves the use of ancient tools and techniques which he will be happy to show visitors to the plant. Cheese making here has never been mechanized or particularly modernized. The shop itself features Crowley Cheese, of course, and maple syrup, honey, jams, jellies, home baked breads, cookies, doughnuts, and Vermont crafts such as pottery, hand blown glass, woolen items, crocheted items, toys, dolls, doll furniture, boats and trucks, ceramic and marble jewelry, wrought iron hooks, stone sculpture, a wide variety of books about Vermont by Vermonters, quilts, carved birds, and more. The gift shop and the cheese factory are in two separate buildings (2 miles apart) and the factory is closed Sundays.

- **JACKSONVILLE.** *Stone Soldier Pottery.* Connie Burnell. 802-368-7077. Open Mon.–Sat. 10–5, Sun. 12–5. This shop features a variety of crafts including functional pottery, weaving, fiber arts, stoneware, jewelry, leather, macrame, woodworking, stained glass, metalwork, blown glass, and sculpture. Pottery is made on the premises by Robert Burnell. The shop is located in the old North River Hall, formerly the town hall for the area.

- **LUDLOW.** *Baker's Village Barn Antiques.* T. T. and M. S. Baker. 57 Depot St. 802-228-4461. Open May–Nov. daily except Sun. 10–5. The Bakers specialize in lamps, silver dolls, tin, china, and glass.

Green Mountain Sugar House. Marjorie and David Harlow.

Rt. 100. 802-228-7151. Open daily June–Oct. 9–6, other times Fri.–Sun. 9–6. The Harlows were southern Vermont's largest producers of maple syrup in 1977. Visitors can watch the syrup being made in the early spring. In addition to maple products, the shop carries Vermont cheese, jams, jellies, other Vermont foods, wooden ware, stone jewelry, soapstone utensils, buckskin gloves, moccasins, macrame, baskets, hand-knitting, and wooden toys. During strawberry season the Harlows' acres of strawberries are open for pick-your-own berries or pre-picked. They have a cider-making operation in the fall.

• **PROCTORSVILLE**. *Proctorsville Pottery*. Alan A. Regin. Twenty Mile Stream Rd. (call for driving instructions). 802-226-7331. Open July 4–Labor Day Fri.–Sun. 10–6 and by appointment. Alan makes a variety of functional pottery which he hopes "realizes its intended function and, at the same time, is interesting to look at and pleasant to hold." His work, which is decorated with a variety of matte glazes, includes bowls, pitchers, planters, teapots, cups, vases, creamers and sugarers.

• **PUTNEY**. *Basketville*. Rt. 5. Open daily all year. Basketville claims to have the world's largest selection of baskets, buckets, and woodenware. Most of the stock is made by their own factory and the remainder is imported. The locally made baskets are woven of white ash and red oak, some using forms that were used more than a century ago.

• **QUECHEE**. *Vermont Craft Exposition*. Craft Professionals of Vermont (CPV). Quechee Country Club. 802-888-2417. This show, held in August, is open to CPV members and both slides and actual works are judged. The Craft Professionals also sponsor an Annual Trade Exposition and Sale at Quechee in April.

• **ROCKINGHAM**. *The Vermont Country Store*. Vrest, Mildred, and Lyman Orton. Rt. 103. Open all year Mon.–Sat. 9–6. Arriving at this store is half the fun, as you drive through a covered bridge to reach it. The store is an offshoot of the Vermont Country Store in Weston, VT (which see) and carries the same high quality line of old fashioned merchandise and food products. The store was designed by Mr. Orton to have the feeling of an old-fashioned store but was built using modern construction methods, to meet the store and museum needs. Most visitors do not realize that the building is a new one, as the old-fashioned feeling is pervasive. Part of the fun of stopping here is visiting the old mill and museum that are part of the operation and seeing the Rodgers statuette collection and many other items.

- **SAXTONS RIVER**. *Schoolhouse Antiques*. Sandy Saunders and Faith Boone. Rt. 121. 802-869-2332. Open all year. Call first in the winter; other seasons 10–5. This shop has country antiques including cherry, pine, and birch drop-leaf tables, one-drawer stands, pine cupboards, corner cupboards, trunks, paintings, baskets, and chairs. Recent offerings included a cobbler's bench ($180), a set of six fiddleback caned chairs ($300), and a 7-foot oak deacon's bench ($400). The owners avoid glass, china, and silver.
- **SPRINGFIELD**. *Fraser's Antiques*. Bob and Mary Fraser. Rt. 143. 802-885-4838. Open daily by chance or by appointment. The Frasers carry a line of New England antiques which generally are left in "as found" condition. Among their specialties are country furniture, early iron, stoneware, textiles, woodenware, toys, baskets, tools, coin, silver, and kitchenware. Recent offerings included a country store coffee grinder ($225), a set of four arrowback side chairs ($375), and an early 1800s sampler ($135). They avoid art glass and formal furniture. The shop is located in a weathered barnlike structure on a former sheep pasture with a view of the Connecticut River.
- **TOWNSHEND**. *Mary Meyer Factory Store*. Rt. 30. 802-365-7793. Open: summer and fall, daily 9–4:30; winter and spring, Mon.–Fri. 9–4:30. Mary Meyer is a leading manufacturer of stuffed toys, musical toys, and puppets. The company was originally formed in New York City but "retired" to Vermont where it has expanded considerably. The diverse stock is available at the factory store with discontinued toys at 25 percent off and seconds at 30 percent off. The shop is ½ mile from the Scott Covered Bridge, longest single-span covered bridge in the state.
- **WINDSOR**. *Vermont State Craft Center at Windsor Annual Festival*. Tricia Nolan. Vermont State Craft Center. 802-674-6729.

This July show is jury-screened and is open to Vermont residents.

Vermont State Craft Center at Windsor House. Main St. 802-674-6729. Open Mon.–Sat. 10–5. The State Craft Center is located in an historic building (Windsor House) that was built in 1840 and saved from demolition in 1971. The building currently houses both the craft center and Vermont Public Radio. The craft center is the marketplace for more than two hundred Vermont craftspeople who display all forms of crafts including weaving, blown-glass, pottery, batik, leather, woodwork, pewter, and jewelry. They also sponsor many arts and crafts classes and workshops. All craftspeople are displayed only after approval by a jury of professionals in the field.

NORTHWESTERN

- **ADDISON**. *Old Stone House Antique Shop*. Walter and Helen Washburn. Just off Rt. 22A. 802-759-2134. Open all year by chance or by appointment. The Old Stone House is a late eighteenth-century stone building. It was built of stones from an old local fort and was fully restored, along with many of the farm outbuildings, by Mr. and Mrs. Washburn after their retirement. The adjoining lake has swans, ducks, and geese. The shop carries a wide range of antiques including Oriental, hooked, and braided rugs, Staffordshire figurines, pressed glass, paintings, furniture, lamps, candle sticks, clocks of all sizes, pewter, silver, brass, copper, tin, iron, wooden primitives, old tools, dolls, quilts, and more.

- **BRANDON**. *Agnes and Bill Franks Antiques*. 55 Franklin St. 802-247-3690. Open all year daily 10–6. The Frankses offer a selection of country furniture including some original painted pieces and some primitives, as well as items of folk art, quilts, baskets, and coverlets. Recent offerings included a blanket chest with old blue paint ($135), and a New England walnut, snake-foot candlestand ($165). The shop is in a small, attractive nineteenth-century farmhouse restored by the owners.

Brandon has a total of twelve antique shops in the village and in the immediate surrounding area and sponsors an *Annual Antique Fair* at Town Hall, the first weekend in August.

- **BURLINGTON**. *Annual Member's Exhibition*. Green Mountain Weavers. Park-McCullough House. This Green Mountain Weavers show is held in March. Check local papers or with the Chamber of Commerce for further information.
- **CAMBRIDGE**. *Cambridge Smithy*. Peter A. Krusch. Fletcher Rd. 802-644-5358. Open Mon.–Fri. 8–5 and by appointment. Mr. Krusch makes a variety of items from wrought iron. He produces other metalwork that includes sculpture and copper items.
- **CHARLOTTE**. *The Chestnut Tree*. Judith H. Pascal. Greenbush Rd. and Rt. 7. 802-425-2811. Open all year daily from 9–5 or by appointment. This shop carries primitives, country furniture, quilts and baskets, as well as other collectibles. Ms. Pascal avoids oak, memorabilia, and glassware. Recent offerings included a large early Canadian cupboard with original red paint ($895), a pine drop-leaf table with drawer ($350), and a blue Hamaden Oriental rug, 3 × 6 ($225). This shop is located at the oldest nursery in the state, F. H. Horsford Nursery, in an 1890 farmhouse.
- **CORNWALL**. *Cornwall Crafts*. Nancy and Spencer Wright. Rt. 30. (3 mi. south of Middlebury). 802-462-2438. Open daily 10–5 (except Mon. Jan.–May). The shop specializes in handcrafted Early American reproduction furniture such as hutches and trestle tables, and Vermont handcrafts including the shop's own popular hobby horse, and pottery. The shop is in a hand-hewn barn (c. 1840) with five rooms and a view of the Green Mountains behind it.
- **FERRISBURG**. *Dakin Farm*. Rt. 7 (between Burlington and Middlebury). 802-425-2448. Open daily all year. Dakin Farm is best known for three Vermont products they sell from their 130-acre farm site. They sell over 26 thousand cans of maple syrup, 10 tons of cheese, and vast amounts of cob-smoked ham and bacon each year, as well as many other farm-type products.
- **GRANVILLE**. *Je-Mel Wood Products*. Melvin Mishkit. Rt. 100. 802-767-3266. Open daily all year 8–6. This outlet features Je-Mel's own wooden ware, including bowls, salt and pepper shak-

ers, salad forks, trays, fireplace bellows, candle holders, etc., as well as maple products and deerskin gloves. Most items are available as firsts or as seconds at discount prices.

Vermont Wood Specialties. William and Jim Parrish. Rt. 100. 802-767-5237. Open daily 9–5 except Christmas and New Year. This shop is the outlet for a variety of woodenware made on the premises, as well as maple products and other gifts. Factory seconds on woodenware are available at discounts from 35–40 percent. Visitors may watch woodenware being made.

● **JEFFERSONVILLE**. *Annual Arts, Crafts, and Antiques Show and Sale*. This is held each fall during the foliage season in October.

● **JERICHO**. *Old Mill Craft Shop*. Jericho Historical Society. Rt. 15. 802-899-3225. Open daily Apr.–Dec. and Wed., Sat. and Sun. Jan.–Mar. 10–5 weekdays, 1–5 Sun. The shop is in the old Chittenden Mills–Old Red Mill which was declared a National Historic Site in 1972. The mill dates from the mid-1850s and has been renovated by the Historical Society which also plans to rebuild the pond so that the mill will be able to generate power again. The mill currently serves as a craft outlet with quilts, paintings, prints, jewelry, pottery, knits, and wooden toys. The shop specializes in items using authentic Bentley snowflake design; W. A. Bentley, who photographed snow crystals, had lived in Jericho.

● **MIDDLEBURY**. *Frog Hollow Annual Crafts Festival*. Vermont State Craft Center at Frog Hollow. 802-388-4871. The Crafts Show is open to Vermont residents, and is juried by actual works. It is held in August.

The Vermont State Craft Center at Frog Hollow. Frog Hollow Rd. 802-388-4871. Open May–Dec. Mon.–Sat. 10–5; Feb.–Apr. Tues.–Sat. 10–5. Closed January. Frog Hollow is a nonprofit organization devoted to the display and sale of the work of more than 250 of Vermont's finest craftspeople. In addition, the center provides craft workshops and quality craft instruction to the community and to school children on a statewide basis. Selections here include quilts, hand-blown glass, hand-woven shawls, wooden boxes, and pottery. The shop is operated in an old mill. Plans are under way to restore the flume and the old mill next door so that the center once again will use waterpower. The center also has a gallery with permanent and changing collections.

The Village Store of Middlebury. Ted and Jean Panicucci. Rt. 7 South. 802-388-6476. Open year-round Mon.–Sat. 9–5:30. This shop specializes in country furniture, primitives, lamps and lighting, iron, tin, copper, brass, baskets, woodenware, quilts, and paintings. Recent offerings included a two-drawer lift top blanket chest, old blue paint, c. 1800 ($350), snake foot, tilt-top candle stand, cherry, c. 1810 ($250), and an eighteenth-century armchair rocker with old red paint ($200).

● **MORRISVILLE**. *The Pines Antiques.* Joan E. Kaiser. Cadys Falls Rd. (follow signs off Rt. 100, south of Morrisville). 802-888-4066. Open May–Oct. by chance or appointment. This shop carries a general line with specialties of early glass, early pottery, ironstone, tin, and early American children's glass dishes. Among their recent offerings were a spongeware pin bank ($40), a Sandwich canary glass lamp ($200), a Shaker bed ($245) and a Shaker spice box ($65). They also have some "dirty barn stuff" and a selection of period furniture. Ms. Kaiser also sponsors winter shows at the Charlmont Restaurant, write RFD #3, Box 143, Morrisville, VT 05661 for details.

● **RIPTON**. *Bread Loaf Mountain Antiques.* Mildred Inskip. Off Rt. 125 at War Memorial. (make a left over bridge ⅛ mi.). 802-388-2436. Open July–Oct. by chance or appointment. This shop has a wide variety of small country antiques including folk art, china, glass, toys, utensils, tools, brass, pewter, tin, candlemolds and some country furniture.

● **SOUTH BURLINGTON**. *Eastern Mountain Sports.* 100 Dorset St. 802-864-0473. Open Mon.–Sat. 9–9.

● **STOWE**. *Annual Stowe Craft Show and Sale.* Stowe League of Women Voters. This Craft Show is held annually in August at the Stowe Elementary School. It is an open show, where slides of works are judged.

Beckerhoff in Stowe. Helen Beckerhoff. Main St. (Rt. 100). 802-253-7668. Open daily 10–6. This is a shop which specializes in fine jewelry, much of it in gold and silver. The shop also has timepieces, glass, crystal, and porcelain figurines. The jewelry offered is made by Ms. Beckerhoff and by several other artisans. The shop, which has a fireplace, is in a late eighteenth-century house, remodelled in 1977.

Samara. Lynn W. Miles. Mountain Rd. (Rt. 108). 802-253-8318. Samara has works of over 100 artisans in virtually all media. In addition to the crafts in the shop, Samara offers a number of made-to-order specialties such as quilts.

The Stowe Pottery. Jean Paul Patnode. Rt. 108. 802-253-4693. Open year-round daily except Sun. 9–5. This shop carries functional and decorative pottery, plates, mugs, bottles, vases, goblets, bowls, candle holders, tea pots, etc., all produced by the potter-owner. The house is almost a hundred years old and was the village blacksmith shop until the 1940s.

Village Artisans. Pond St. 802-253-8068. Open daily 10–5. This shop is owned and operated by five craftspeople, some of whom demonstrate their craft to visitors. Included in their offerings are wooden bowls, art, toys, pottery, wrought iron, and quilts.

● **VERGENNES**. *Kennedy Brothers*. Swisspot Building. Rt. 100. 802-877-2975. Factory open Mon.–Fri.; gift shop open daily all year. Both open 9–5:30. Kennedy Brothers has established a reputation as a manufacturer of a variety of woodenware. During the week visitors to the factory-shop can watch these items being made through three large picture windows. The woodenware sold in the shop is available at 25 percent off list for first-quality items, and 50 percent or more off for discontinued or second-quality items. The gift shop has a wide selection of pottery, glass, wood, and other items for sale.

● **WAITSFIELD**. *Millhouse Gallery*. David Millstone. Rt. 100. 802-296-2206. Open daily, 11–11. The gallery handles a range of hand-crafts including jewelry, pottery, paintings, and sculpture. The gallery is associated with a restaurant of the same name and both are housed in a two-story wooden building with hand-hewn beams which span the upper level. The building was originally a Methodist Church and was built in 1835.

● **WATERBURY CENTER**. *Sunshine Snowy Day*. John H. Wetmore. Rt. 100. (3 mi. south of Stowe). Open Wed.–Sat. 10–5.

This shop carries a general line of Vermont crafts and Ashley wood stoves. Among the crafts displayed recently in the shop were gold jewelry by owner, ceramic dinnerware, and other stoneware by Peter Wendland and wooden toys by Bill Smith.

NORTHEASTERN

• **BRADFORD**. *South Road Pottery*. Phyllis and Bruce Murray. South Rd. (call for directions). 802-222-5758. Open daily 10–5 except Jan. This shop is devoted to pottery and paintings and specializes in tiles, vases, teapots, pitchers, oil and electric lamps, creamers and sugarers, espresso cups, bowls, jars, and watercolors and drawings by Lee W. Katzenbach. Typical of pottery prices are mugs for $6 each and a four-cup tea set for $36. The shop is located on a nineteenth-century farm with its sheds in the foothills of the Green Mountains overlooking the White Mountains of New Hampshire.

• **CABOT**. *Cabot Farmers' Cooperative*. Follow signs from Rt. 2 or Rt. 15. Open year-round Mon.–Fri. 8–4:30, Sat. May–Nov. The Cabot Farmers' Cooperative is New England's largest manufacturer of cheddar cheese and butter. Visitors may watch through picture windows the manufacture of this particular type of Vermont cheddar. The shop offers good buys in cheese and other dairy products.

The Craft Shop at Molly's Pond. Martha Price and Luella Schroeder. U.S. 2. Open May–Dec. daily except Sun. Summer hours: 10:30–5:30, fall and winter: 1–5:30. This shop represents a variety of Vermont artists-craftspeople who produce stained glass, blown glass, stoneware, ceramic wheel-thrown sculpture, wood block print posters, silk screened prints and the jewelry of co-owner Luella Schroeder.

• **DERBY LINE**. *Tranquil Things*. Patricia and Richard Wright. 43 Main St. 802-873-3454. Open Mon.–Sat. 10–5. The Wrights carry a selection of textile crafts (some by Patricia), graphics, jewelry, woodworking and carving, stained glass, wind chimes, kites, folk records, books, baskets, hand-dyed and stitched clothing and, courtesy of the Shetland Shop, Irish capes and Scottish cashmere sweaters.

● **EAST BARRE**. *Farr's Antiques*. Edward Farr. Rt. 110. 802-476-4308. Open all year by chance or appointment. This shop specializes in items used in Vermont homes in the 1800s. It carries Victorian and country furniture, glass, china, primitives, advertising, dolls, utensils, tools, brass, tin, prints, quilts, and clocks. Recent offerings included kerosene lamps ($20–$300), a one-drawer blanket chest, all original ($350), and a round oak table with claw feet ($300). The shop avoids imports and reproductions and is located in a Vermont farmhouse and barn (hand-hewn, original condition) dating from c. 1850.

● **EAST BURKE**. *Art Cache*. Bottom of Darling Hill. 802-626-5711. The Art Cache sponsors special shows of Vermont artists several times a year. The Annual Spring Show is usually held in April and the Annual Outdoor Exhibition and Sale of Paintings is held there each September.

● **GREENSBORO**. *The Miller's Thumb*. Gertrude Corwin. 802-533-2960. Open late June–Labor Day, Mon.–Sat. 10–5. The Miller's Thumb carries hand crafts, mostly of Vermont origin of a wide variety of types and media including Woodbury's woodenware, Kennedy stoneware, Bennington pottery, Woodbury pewter and the work of Helen Beckerhoff, Hazel Rochester, Michael Boylen, and others. The shop is located in a restored Grist Mill, painted barn red. There is a viewing window in the floor permitting a look at the millstream cascading below.

● **JOHNSON**. *Johnson Woolen Mills, Inc*. Main St. (Rt. 15 between Cambridge and Morrisville). 802-635-2271. Open year-round Mon.–Fri. 8–5, Sat. 9–4. Closed Sun. The mill has been at this site since 1842. It offers blankets, hunting clothes, yard goods, loden coats, chamois shirts and more at mill prices.

● **LOWER WATERFORD**. *Waterford Hills Antiques*. Mr. and Mrs. Roger Olds. Highway 19. 802-748-9456. Open May 30 to November 1 daily 9–6; other times by chance or appointment. The Oldses carry a wide range of general antiques covering several periods. However they are particularly interested in lamps (early periods to Victorian and including Tiffany) and country pine furniture. The shop also has many New England primitives with accessories, kitchenwares, paper antiques, advertising items, textiles and a selection of glass and china. Recent offerings included a complete, all original Gone-with-the-Wind lamp ($175), primitive portrait of a small boy, oil ($200), and an early country cheese press, complete with accessories ($225).

- **MONTPELIER**. *Annual Fall Festival of Vermont Crafts*. This is held each October. Call the Chamber of Commerce for exact dates and details at 802-223-2441.

Weaver's Web. Christine Abrams. 39 Barre St. 802-223-6889. Open Tues.–Sat. 10–5. Weaver's Web is a working weaving production studio which manufactures handwoven bags, stoles, scarfs, pillows, and throws. The weavers also do commission work and reproductions. The store is a retail outlet for weaving and knitting supplies, looms, and equipment and is located in an old Victorian house next to the oldest house in Montpelier.

- **NEWBURY**. *Valmont View Antiques*. Dorothy Ebeling. Main St. 802-866-5639. Open June 15 to October 15 Mon.–Sat. 10–5. This shop specializes in New England town and country items including eighteenth- to early twentieth-century clocks (American shelf, wall, and tall case), lighting devices (candles, whale oil, kerosene, electrified for hand, table, wall and ceiling), furniture (tables, chairs, chests and cupboards), and furnishings (wood stoves and hearth items, china, porcelain, glass, children's furniture and toys, brass, pewter, copper, tin, iron, wooden utensils and tools, pottery, quilts, advertising articles, pictures and frames). The shop itself is in a lovely attached clapboard barn, adjacent to an historic (1790 and 1830) home on the west bank of the Connecticut River with a spectacular view of the White Mountains.

- **PLAINFIELD**. *Annual Goddard College Craft Fair*. Goddard College. 802-454-8311, ext. 308. This Craft Fair is open to residents of Vermont and New England. It is held in August.

- **RANDOLPH CENTER**. *William Dupras*. Main St. 802-728-5571. Open year-round by chance or appointment. Mr. Dupras' antique shop is located in an historic area with several early 1800s brick and wood frame houses in a village on top of a lovely

Vermont hill. He carries early American furniture and accessories including tables, cupboards, hutches, stands, chairs, and a few Victorian pieces. Recent offerings included six rabbit-ear chairs, refinished ($600) and a refinished hutch table ($925). Mr. Dupras avoids jewelry and art glass.

● **ROYALTON**. *The Vermont Sugar House, Inc*. Jct. Rts. 14 and 107. 802-763-8809. Open daily Mar.–Dec. 9–6. This shop carries a full line of maple products, Vermont cheese, handcrafts, and pancakes. Sap is boiled at the shop in March and April.

● **STRAFFORD**. *Annual Fair*. Vermont Artisans, Inc. On-the-Green. The Craft Fair is invitational, held in August since 1973.

Vermont Artisans, Inc. On-the-Green. 802-765-9861. Open Wed.–Sun. 11–5, Fri. 6–9. Vermont Artisans are a self-supporting, nonprofit craft center which displays and sells the work of its members who produce virtually every type of hand-crafted item. In addition the center is a gallery, classroom, and pottery studio. They offer free concerts of Renaissance and country music, poetry readings, chess and chamber music evenings, and monthly contra-dances with caller Dudley Laufman. Also featured are weekend craft workshops, village seminars, and summertime crafts fairs and festivals.

● **THETFORD CENTER**. *R. Voake, Toymaker*. Rt. 113. 802-785-2837. Open Mon.–Fri. 10–5, and weekends in summer. R. Voake makes over seventy-five varieties of toys ranging in size from small push toys to large, ridable wooden toys including trains, trucks, boats, rocking horses, riding animals, airplanes, pull carts, play blocks, and many more. All items are made on the premises and visitors can watch the toys being made from native Vermont hardwoods. Toys purchased here are available at 40 percent below their retail price.

New Hampshire

SHOPPERS FOR CRAFTS in New Hampshire should be particularly pleased with the offerings of the League of New Hampshire Craftsmen, an organization with about 4500 members and a number of nonprofit craft centers around the state. Most independent crafts shops are members of this organization. Furthermore, the New Hampshire Antiques Dealers Association is a very strong organization and has done much to improve the quality of antique-shopping in this state.

For the convenience of readers, the shops and outlets in New Hampshire are listed here by the six regions recommended by the state—-Monadnock, Merrimack Valley, Seacoast, Dartmouth–Lake Sunapee, Lakes, and White Mountains. Within each region, the towns are arranged alphabetically.

Before leaving for New Hampshire, we recommend getting travel help from the State Department of Economic Development, P.O. Box 856, State House Annex, Concord, NH 03301. Also helpful is the literature from each of the regional associations. Ask the state for a list if you plan to spend some time in any one region.

MONADNOCK REGION

● **AMHERST**. *Cricket Farm Antiques*. Lyna C. Mueller. Boston Post Rd. (2 mi. south of the village). 603-673-4154. Open every day, by chance. This shop carries antiques and works of art with

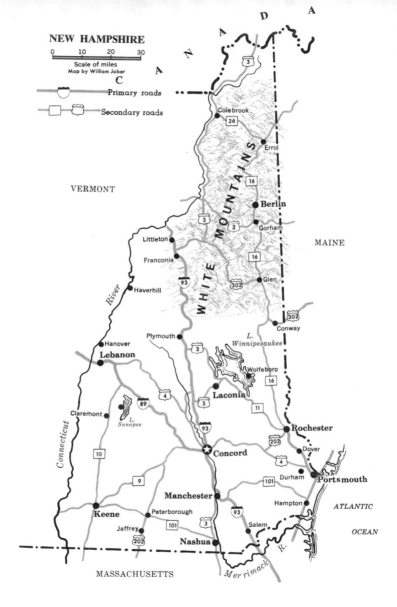

NEW HAMPSHIRE

0 10 20 30
Scale of miles
Map by William Jaber

Primary roads
Secondary roads

CANADA

VERMONT

MAINE

WHITE MOUNTAINS

Colebrook
26
Errol
16
Berlin
Gorham
2
Littleton
Franconia
16
93
302
Glen
Haverhill
302
Conway
Plymouth
L. Winnipesaukee
Hanover
3
Lebanon
Laconia
Wolfeboro
16
Claremont
L. Sunapee
89
4
11
3
10
93
Rochester
202
Dover
9
Concord
4
Durham
Portsmouth
101
Manchester
Hampton
Peterborough
93
ATLANTIC
Keene
Salem
OCEAN
Jaffrey
101
3
202
Nashua
Merrimack R.

Connecticut River

MASSACHUSETTS

the emphasis on eighteenth-century porcelain, art glass, and period furniture. The shop is air conditioned in the summer and heated in the winter. Featured recently were a small, bow-front, inlayed, Hepplewhite-period New Hampshire sideboard ($3,400); a small, six-board-tall blanket chest with one drawer ($175); a marked New Hall cup and saucer ($65); and a cottage chair ($25). The shop is situated in a big red barn.

Outdoor Antiques Market. Betty Douglas. Rt. 122 (4 mi. south of village). 603-673-2093. Open late Apr.–Oct. Sun. 8–4. More than two hundred exhibitors come here every Sunday. It is a well-known long established market in a lovely country setting of more than 20 acres. The many antique displays are set up under large shade trees. There is an admission charge of 50¢ per person, children free. The market provides free parking and snack bars are plentiful. As an added attraction, on the last Sunday of every month there is an Antique Auto Swap and Sell Meet. The emphasis here is on antiques and collectibles.

• **ANTRIM**. *The Nook and Cranny*. William Lewan. Rt. 31. (2 mi. from Rt. 9 or 3 mi. from Rt. 202). 603-588-2253. Open all year by chance or appointment. The Nook and Cranny carries early and country furniture and accessories.

• **HANCOCK**. *The Cobbs*. Charles M. and Dudley G. Cobb. Old Dublin Rd. 603-525-4053. Open every day, by chance or by appointment. To get to this shop one must take the unmarked road between the schoolhouse and the cemetery off Rt. 123, ¼ mile southwest of the village. This shop does not accept any antiques made before 1820 and has a line that includes both furniture and accessories. Included in the collection are Queen Anne and Chippendale period pieces, fire place iron, early needlework, brass candlesticks, woodenware, baskets, some paintings, early pottery, glass, china, and Oriental rugs. Recently the shop offered a set of four Country Queen Anne side chairs ($4800), a maple and pine gate-leg table ($2500), a walnut slant-front desk ($2150) and a mushroom slat-back arm chair ($1100). The shop is located in a typical 1790 Cape Cod house with an outstanding room painted with scenes by Rufus Porter. The house is set on 21 acres of beautiful rolling countryside.

Hardings of Hancock. Mrs. Vincent Harding. Depot St. 603-525-3518. Open by chance or appointment seven days a week. Mrs. Harding carries a line of antiques that includes country furniture, early lighting, hand-forged ironware, brass, copper, woodenware, period andirons, primitive accents, and early tools. Recently she had an early eighteenth-century cradle ($850), an early hand-forged pricket lamp ($450), and a collection of iron cooking utensils ($15–$125). The shop overlooks the much photographed Norway Pond.

● **HILLSBORO CENTRE**. *Old Dunbar House*. Ralph C. Stuart. Center Rd. 603-464-3937. Open all year, by chance or by appointment. Mr. Stuart carries only period antiques with no offerings of items made after 1830. Most representative of his antiques are his selections of pewter, Chinese export items, and period furniture made of native New Hampshire woods. His recent offerings included a selection of period maple and birch chests (some at $550, most higher); a period corner cupboard ($800) and a pine tavern table ($600). The shop is in the old Dunbar House, built in 1778. This was the home of the second doctor in the town and has lovely trees planted in 1856, fine gardens, and a nice greenhouse.

● **KEENE**. *Douglas Cuddle Toys Factory Store*. Douglas Co. Inc. 222 West St. 603-352-3414. Open year-round Mon.–Sat. 9–5. The Factory Store sells stuffed animals at discounted prices. The toys, of top quality, are particularly well suited for young children. There are musical toys, chime animals, hand puppets, and licensed characters—it is the home of Dr. Suess's Cat in the Hat. The regular first quality merchandise is sold at 10 percent off retail and specials are discounted up to 50 percent. The factory store is located in an old mill complex that has been recently restored and now houses, in addition to Cuddle Toys, Country Artisans, Village Woodsmiths and Keene Mill End Store (see **Mill Village, Keene, NH**).

Mill Village. West and Island Sts. Mill Village is a factory complex of old buildings which have been restored and now house several shops and factory outlets. Country Artisans is a gallery and outlet for artists and craftspeople. The business also conducts classes in arts and crafts. Craftspeople can be seen at work on the premises. Some of the crafts include: puppets, pottery, patchwork, leaded glass, terrariums, leather, silversmithing, antique restoration, hand-printed fabrics, and children's clothing, phone 603-357-3120. The Keene Mill End Store sells all sorts of fabrics for clothing, upholstery, and drapery, phone 603-352-9844. The Village Woodsmith features woodcarving of signs, candle holders, clocks, and wall plaques by Art Ritchie. He specializes in custom carving. There is also a furniture repair and Bix furniture stripping and refinishing operation, phone 603-357-4040. Cuddle Toys Factory Outlet is located here.

Dale Pregent Antiques. 142 Marlboro St. (center of town). 603-352-6736. Open year-round by chance or appointment. Dale Pregent carries a general line of antiques including country and formal furniture, pewter, historical soft paste, and small primitives. The shop avoids oak.

• **MARLOW.** *Sand Pond Antique and Gun Shop.* James and Gaye Tillinghast. Sand Pond Rd. (3 mi. north on Rt. 10 from village, then ¾ mi. up Sand Pond). 603-446-3460. Open all year daily 10–5 (except Tues. by appointment only). The Tillinghasts sell a general line of antiques, but specialize in old tools, bottles, antique guns and ammunition, pottery, paper ephemera, any advertising and postal history. They have one of the largest selections of antique ammunition in the world. Recently they had a large collection of spool cabinets.

• **MILFORD.** *Kee Pon Truckin' Company.* Bob Farrow and Lee Farrow. 8 Millbrook Dr. 603-673-5286. Open by chance or by appointment. This shop offers handcrafted wooden toys, particularly various types of trucks, and hand-embroidered, custom designed clothing. Most clothing is denim, including jackets and various styles of shirts and blouses.

Pine Shed Antiques. Cynthia and Jim Forsyth. Elm St. (Rt. 101 West). 603-673-2167. Open all year by chance or appointment. The Pine Shed specializes in jewelry, dolls, and old clothing but also carries a general line including furniture, glass, and china. Recently they had a Queen Anne drop-leaf table signed T. Moulton ($2500); a Chinese table ($550); and a brass piano lamp ($290).

• **PETERBOROUGH**. *Brookstone*. Vose Farm Road. 603-924-7181. Open Jan.–June Mon.–Sat. 9–5, July–Dec. daily 9–5. Closed Thanksgiving and Christmas. Brookstone gained its reputation as a catalog merchant selling "Hard to find Tools." Their showroom reflects this philosophy and browsers with a leaning toward fine tools and gadgets will find much to content them. Brookstone has recently expanded their offerings to include many kitchen and general "hard to find" gift selections so the appeal of the store has broadened considerably.

The Game Preserve. Lee and Rally Dennis. Spring Rd. (west on Main St. to Windy Row; first left off Windy Row is Spring Rd.). 603-924-6710. Open by chance or appointment year-round. The Game Preserve sells old game duplicates and other small collectibles. The shop is primarily a minimuseum of old board games and card games dating back to 1843. There are more than seven hundred exhibits on the walls. The duplicates and antique items are for sale. The Dennises reputation is in the old American board game, with brilliant lithography on the covers and vintage graphics. Several primitive games and larger old games are set up for actual play. The games date from no later than 1930. Besides the duplicate games, the Dennises sell cards, children's books, postcards, and other paper memorabilia, as well as some tin and wood. Komical Konversation Kards, c. 1910, are $9; Red Riding Hood, 1895, sells for $14. The Game Preserve deals very little in chess, Mah Jongg, cribbage, or checkers. The shop is distinguished by a most unusual hand-carved sign carrying the name of the shop as well as its logo.

Willow Brook Antiques. Mary Warner Hoffman. Wilton Rd. (Rt. 101). 603-924-6836. Open daily all year, 10–5. Willow Brook deals in primitives, tin, iron, fine china, ladder backs, Hitchcock chairs, grain measures, baskets, and hand-hewn wooden pieces. Mary Hoffman also has a selection of antique hats, miniatures, quilts, folk art, rare and second-hand books, and glass. She avoids carnival and depression glass, cameras, and late Victorian. Recently she had a pine cradle c. the 1800s ($150), some Red Ware ($25–$35), and several sizes of unburnished copper kettles ($45–$55).

• **SHARON**. *Sharon Arts Center*. Rt. 123. 603-924-7256.

Open Mon.–Sat. 10–5, mid-April–Dec. Sun. 1–5. The Sharon Arts Center was founded by William and Ruth Young in 1946. The Handcraft Shop, affiliated with the League of New Hampshire Craftsmen, opened a few years after that. The handcraft shop carries a complete line of crafts representing a large number of the many thousand members of the League. In addition to the broad range of crafts available for purchase, the Gallery at the Center features a continuous, changing exhibit of arts and crafts as well as various arts and crafts classes.

- **SOUTH WEARE**. *Harrison House Antiques*. Barbara Harrison. Rt. 77. 603-529-7174. Open daily all year 9–6. The Harrisons' shop carries a line of refinished country furniture with the emphasis on kitchen furniture including piesafes, cupboards and accessories. They also have a good collection of advertising collectibles including a number of signs made from old country store shipping boxes. Recently they had a poplar piesafe from Ohio with pierced tin all around, a 6-ft. Deacon's bench in original condition, and a wall coffee grinder with original glass. They avoid glass, china, silver, jewelry, and guns. The shop is located in a restored barn attached to their 1783 house.

- **SPOFFORD**. *The Stone House*. Gordon Chamberlin. Jct. Rts. 9 and 63. 603-363-4616. Open year-round by chance or appointment. This lovely shop carries a selection of stoneware, glass, fabrics, soft paste, and Staffordshire china, flint glass, and early hand-made fabrics. In addition, Mr. Chamberlin carries a selection of early furniture in as-found condition. Recently he had a small Queen Ann walnut highboy with newer brasses ($2300), a Somerset early water cooler incised with two birds ($1500), a fifteen-piece Leeds tea set ($600), a painting of a young boy ($1000), and a three-piece blue Staffordshire teapot, sugarer and creamer ($250). The beautiful granite building that houses the shop was built in 1831 as a tavern and has the original cage-type bar, ten fireplaces and a second floor ballroom with fiddlers' bench. The third floor has cubicles with built-in bunks where the drivers and coachmen slept.

- **WALPOLE**. *Kirk-Lamothe Gallery and Cheshire Crafts Shop*. Anne Kirk-Lamothe. Main St. (exit 5 off Rt. 91). 603-756-

3234. Open May–Christmas, Tues.–Sat. 12:30–4. The Kirk-Lamothe Gallery features arts and crafts of area craftspeople along with antiques. Anne carries functional and decorative pottery, furniture, graphics, painting, stoneware, jewelry, leather, knitting, woodworking, stained glass, quilts, and stuffed animals—especially cats. The shop recently had a 70 × 90 braided rug ($150), a hand-made quilt ($150), many different stuffed cats ($1.50–$15), and hand-screened cards (50¢ each). The gallery and shop are in a large Victorian house built by Senator Hastings in 1865. The building also houses The Peacock Shop which carries only fine women's clothes.

• **WEST SWANZEY**. *Homestead Woolen Mill Store*. G. K. Brown and Sons. Winchester St. (Rt. 10). 603-352-2023. Open weekdays 9–5, Sat. 9–3. Closed Sun. The Woolen Mill Store sells polyester, 100 percent wool, wool and nylon, wool and polyester, rug ends, camp blankets, and throws at discounted prices. Remnants sell for $1.50 a yard. The store is located in a nineteenth-century textile factory that was remodeled in 1977.

Knotty Pine Antiques. Joan E. Papas. Rt. 10. (5 mi. from Keene). 603-352-5252. Open seven days a week all year 10–5. This is an enormous antique mall with booths for 65 to 70 dealers under one roof. They carry everything, ranging in price from $1 up including primitives, tools, china, glassware, jewelry, small furniture, pottery, brass, and much more.

• **WILTON**. *Aurora Farm Antiques*. Jean M. Eckhardt. Captain Clark Rd. (1½ miles off Rt. 101, west of Wilton). 603-654-9294. Open all year by chance or by appointment. Ms. Eckhardt carries a general line with the emphasis on furniture, prints, and paintings. Recent offerings included a T. J. Bailey painting of a street scene in the snow ($80); a Chinese scatter rug, c. 1920 ($200); and a corner cupboard—all original except finish, nineteenth-century, with glazed door above and panelled door below ($450). The owner says she avoids no specific group of antiques but is not particularly strong on glass, especially art glass or depression glass. The shop is in the summer kitchen and former woodshed of an eighteenth-century Colonial house in a tranquil country setting high on a hill with a spectacular view of Lyndeborough and Monadnock. Sheep graze on a nearby pasture.

MERRIMACK VALLEY REGION

- **BEDFORD**. *Bell Hill Antiques*. Rt. 101. 603-472-5580.
Open·every day 10–5:30. Bell Hill is a group of seventeen dealers
who offer country and formal furniture, paintings, quilts, tin and
woodenware, toys, dolls, folk art, tools, some jewelry and some
silver. The shops are in the Houck Real Estate Building.
- **CANTERBURY**. *Canterbury Fair*. Off I-93 on Rt. 106. End
of July. The Canterbury Fair is now in its twentieth year and offers
antiques booths, an auction, crafts sales and demonstrations, old-
fashioned dancing and country music, a barbeque, and much more.
Admission and parking are free.
- **CHESTER**. *Olde Chester Antiques*. Betty and Barney
Priest. Raymond Rd. 603-887-4778. Open May 1–Nov. 1 10–5, and
by appointment. The Priests carry country furniture and accessories dating before 1825. The furniture has the original milk paint
or other finish, where possible. Recent offerings included an all-
original schoolmaster's desk on stretcher base with drawers, a
one-drawer tap table with scrubbed top and early red base, and a
set of four ladderback chairs in untouched condition. They avoid
glass, china, and later furniture.
- **CONCORD**. *Antique Show*. Convention Hall. New Hampshire Highway Hotel. Mid-August. The Antique Show is held
under the auspices of The New Hampshire Antique Dealers Association and the New Hampshire Historical Society. It is a three-
day event in mid-August. There is an admission charge. For
schedule and information write New Hampshire Antique Dealers
Association, Ralph K. Reed (Sec.), Pleasant Valley, RFD 1, Wolfeboro, NH 03894. Enclose a stamped, self-addressed legal-sized envelope and they will send the current directory of dealers and the
show times and dates.

Concord Arts and Crafts. 36 North Main St. 603-338-8171.
Open Mon.–Thurs. 10–5, Fri. 10–5:30, and Sat. 9–5. The shop

sells only hand-made items produced by New Hampshire craftspeople. A wide variety of crafts in an assortment of media exhibited and sold. Some of the featured craftspeople are Dudley Giberson, glass; Gerry Williams, potter; Vivika and Otto Heino, potters; and Ruth Springer, weaver. A handwoven rug (5 × 7) recently sold for $350, a stained-glass stand-up mirror (7½″ × 9″) was $15, and a small wooden cheese spreader, $3.50.

- **CONTOOCOOK**. *Buckeye House Antiques*. Craig and Nancy Cheney. Maple St. (Rt. 127). 603-746-5037. Open all year by chance or appointment. Buckeye House features a small, ever changing stock of quality antique country furniture and accessories. It also has a collection of folk art. The antiques are displayed in an early nineteenth-century home. Recently the Cheneys had a large cheese basket with handles ($150), a cupboard with the original old blue paint ($325), and a tiger maple chest of drawers ($475). The Cheneys avoid glass, china, dolls, junky collectibles, watches, clocks, and postcards.

- **DERRY**. *The Old Emery Place*. Julian Hayes. 27 South Main St. (at the town rotary go south on Rt. 28 bypass). 603-432-9640. Open Mar.–Nov. daily 10–4, and by appointment other times. Julian Hayes handles a general line of antiques which feature paper memorabilia, glass, china, tin, woodenware and furniture. He also has some paintings, old books, advertising art, and postcards. The shop has *no* guns, coins, or jewelry. It is located in a c. 1800s hand-hewn barn and shed.

- **EPSOM**. *The Betty House*. Charles and Philip Yeaton. North Rd. (½ mi. off Rt. 4). 603-736-9087. Open by chance or appointment when the snow is not too deep. The Yeatons' principal interest is early American primitives, kitchen utensils, and tools. They carry a variety of other antiques and near antiques including a large selection of furniture, woodenware, tin, stoneware, and some glass and china. There are some unusual primitives. The stock is housed in four barns which include what was once a cider making house, a farm equipment storage shed, the original house built c. 1800, and a large farm barn. Among their many collections one may find a sausage stuffer ($15), a blueberry rake ($20), an iron donut kettle ($14), and a cottage chest with original stencil ($70).

• **HOPKINTON**. *Meadow Hearth*. John and Robin Howe. Briar Hill (exit 4 off Rt. 89 to village, take road opposite Cracker Barrel). 603-746-3947. Open daily but appointments advised. Meadow Hearth has a reputation for American primitive furniture. They also carry a diversified stock of furniture, toys, portraits, and other paintings. The Howes recently had a Chippendale claw-foot desk ($2700), a pair of Spanish foot chairs ($1300) and a Sheraton bureau ($425). The shop is in a 1790s farm house.

Mitchell's Antiques. Rollins Rd. 603-746-5056. Open all year (heated shop) by chance or appointment. The Mitchell's general line stresses primitives and country furniture as well as folk art, toys, utensils, tools, metalware, tin, quilts, clocks, miniatures. Recent offerings included two cobbler's benches, a blanket chest with original smoke paint and set of six kitchen Windsor chairs. This shop avoids glass, china, silver, guns, coins, and paper.

Old Storey Barn. Nels and Doris Kraemer. Hawthorne Hill Rd. 603-224-0322. Open late April–early November, usually 10–5. The Kraemers carry antiques and collectibles, including old pressed glass (cup plates), coins, old metals, pattern glass, presidential campaign buttons, Haviland Limoges china, coin silver, and both enamel and tin advertising signs. They recently had a hoosier kitchen cabinet ($125), a pewter ice-cream mold ($28), a Sandwich glass cup plate ($16), and a portable brass oil lamp ($30). Their shop is in a rustic old barn on a stone foundation.

Wheat and Chaff Antiques. Wayne and Peg Woodard. Hopkinton Rd. (Rt. 103). 603-746-3313. Open all year by chance or appointment. Wheat and Chaff Antiques features country furniture and accessories, spongeware, early American pattern glass, and quilts. The country furniture includes some period Hepplewhite, dry sinks, stepback cupboards, sea chests, lamp stands, beds, farm tables, and more. The pattern glass is Flint and non-Flint 1830–1880. Quilts are mostly early and Amish. The spongeware is primarily blue and white. The Amish quilts range from $100–$275; a dry sink, $450; farm work table, $275, and a Queen Anne chest on frame, period, $2200. The Woodards' home is a 1780 colonial, and their shop is in the 1780 barn nearby (heated in winter!).

• **LONDONDERRY**. *The Renée Monday Shop*. Renée Blunt

Teas. 198 Mammoth Rd. 603-434-7763. Open all year daily 9–5 and by appointment. Renée carries antiques, collectibles, and memorabilia. She has furniture (some primitives and some Victorian), glass, china, and interesting miscellany. Recently her shop had a cherry drop-leaf table with one drawer ($200), a mini five-drawer pine silver chest ($225), and a pine corner cupboard with four shelves and doors ($400).

● **MANCHESTER**. *Buyers Marketplace*. Sheraton Wayfarer Convention. 603-224-3375. Open March. This show is sponsored by the League of New Hampshire Craftsmen and is a juried show open to craftsmen from New Hampshire, Maine, Vermont, and Massachusetts.

End of the Trail Antiques. June and Fred Kos. 420 and 426 Chestnut St. (two shops, across from the post office). 603-669-1238. Open Mon.–Sat. 10–4. The Koses carry a general line of antiques, memorabilia, and collectibles. They have pine and Victorian furniture and accessories.

Indian Head Athletics. 175 Canal St. 603-627-1292. Open Tues., Wed., Fri. and Sat. 9:30–5:30; Mon. and Thurs. 9:30–9. This outlet sells a complete line of sporting goods including Profile skiwear, Speedo tank suits, Converse athletic shoes and Dexter golf shoes. Typical discounts include leather bowling shoes, regularly $19.95 for $12.95, and Speedo, regularly $15.50 for $8.95. The outlet has three annual sales in February, July, and October and is located in a 100-year-old red brick shoe factory.

Pandora Factory Store. Pandora Industries. Canal and Dow. Sts. (Amoskeag Bridge exit off Eurett Turnpike). 603-668-4802. Open Jan.–May: Mon.–Sat. 9–5:30, Thurs. 9–9, Sun. 10–5. June–Nov. 22: Mon., Thurs., Fri. 9–9, Tues., Wed., Sat. 9–5:30; Sun. 10–5. This factory store carries everything in the Pandora line at savings from 30–50 percent. They feature men's, women's and children's sweaters in an enormous range of sizes, styles, and colors. The store also carries shirts, blouses, slacks, skirts, scarves and hats at the same discounts. Irregular items are marked and the savings on these is more than 50 percent. The store has special big sales on Columbus Day, Veterans Day, a pre-Christmas sale, back-to-school sale, and, in June, an anniversary sale. Several other factory stores are adjacent to Pandora's. The store is housed in the former Manchester Locomotive Works building which built many famous locomotives such as the *Pioneer* from the 1850s to the 1900s. The hand-hewn gigantic overhead beams are still intact and visible. The exterior of the building is maintained as it was in the late 1800s.

Wel-Shoe Company. 168 Amherst St. (next to City Library). 603-668-1724. Open Mon.–Wed. and Fri.–Sat. 9:30–5:30, Thurs. 9:30–9. The Wel-Shoe Company sells ladies' dress, tailored, and casual quality shoes direct from the factory (slight imperfections repaired at the factory) with savings of up to 50 percent of the retail price.

● **MERRIMACK**. *Red Barn Antiques*. Edna Mower and Marian Briggs. Depot St. (200 ft. off Rt. 3). 603-424-5235 or 424-5314. Open on weekends in summer and by appointment in winter. Red Barn offers antiques, collectibles, and memorabilia. It carries furniture (early and Victorian), glassware, tinware, china, quilts, cupboards, crocks, jugs, and ironware. Mrs. Mower and Mrs. Briggs have a variety of cupboards—slanted tops, pyramid tops, double- and single-doors. They also have some tin advertising signs and early 1800s candle stands (iron). They do not deal in bottles or jewelry. The shop is located in a handsome eighteenth-century hand-pegged barn attached to a lovely old two-story brick house where Mrs. Mower lives. The house sports an old fireplace with a beehive oven around which one generally can find family and friends.

● **NASHUA**. *Nashua League of New Hampshire Craftsmen*. Headquarters of the New Hampshire League of Craftsmen, Concord, N.H. 95 West Pearl St. 603-882-4171. Open all year, Mon.–Sat. 9:30–5:30, Thurs. evening until 9 P.M. The League sells and exhibits handcrafted items made in New Hampshire. They have toys, prints, jewelry, blown glass, pottery, weaving, and wood. Sterling silver earrings are $2; a lamp (pottery) and shade, $40; and a stained glass window costs about $450. Some of the craftspeople exhibited are Calvin Libby (prints), Marilyn McCubrey (jewelry), "Salamandra Glass," Derek and Linda Marshall and Gerry Williams (pottery), and Carol T. Lummus (prints).

● **NORTHWOOD**. *The Fianders*. Walter and Ginger Fiander. Rt. 4. 603-942-8114. Open daily all year 9–5. The Fianders carry a general line of antiques and collectibles, stressing furniture, china, and glass. They recently had a royal Vienna hand-painted vase, a royal Bonn hand-painted vase, and an old Tiffany type table lamp. Their shop is in an 1800 colonial barn with hand-hewn beams, mortised and tenoned and pegged together.

Northwood Craftsmens Fair. Northwood Stoneware Pottery. Rt. 202-9 (near Rt. 4). Weekend preceding Labor Day weekend (late August). This show has been held annually since 1973 and currently displays the work of seventy-five local craftspeople. In addition to the crafts sale there are crafts demonstrations and music. Admission is free.

Northwood Stoneware Pottery. Jeff Lalish. Jct. Rts. 202-9 and 4. 603-942-8829. Open Apr.–Dec. 9–5:30 daily and by appointment the rest of the year. This shop carries the work of the owner, Jeff Lalish, who specializes in traditional eighteenth- and nineteenth-century American stoneware, including some reproductions, crocks, and jugs. He also makes porcelain, redware, raku, sculptures, and mirrors. The shop carries the works of other local craftspeople including pottery, some graphic art, ceramic sculpture, and other handcrafts. One gallon decorated crocks are $30 and a 1-gallon jug is $15. The shop is located in the barn and shed portions of a typical late eighteenth-century New England house-with-attached-barn.

● **NOTTINGHAM**. *Bittersweet Farm Antiques*. Benjamin and Grace Hayes. Rt. 4 (halfway between Concord and Portsmouth). 603-942-7017. Open all year 10–5 daily. Bittersweet Farm offers a general line of antiques including furniture, lamps, clocks, and woodenware. The Hayeses specialize in good china and glass. They do not carry bottles or reproductions. A Nippon chocolate set ($85) was among their recent finds, along with an oak gingerbread clock ($150) and a wave crest cracker jar ($125).

● **PELHAM**. *Hartley's Barn*. Mammoth Road (Rt. 128). 603-883-3269. Open by appointment or by chance generally 10–12 and 1–5. Hartley's Barn (a restored eighteenth-century barn) is full of antiques, jewelry, and silverware. Much of the silverware consists of matching service and a registry of it is kept. Recent offerings included a shell cameo brooch with gold frame ($45), an old coin silver ladle, c. 1850 ($30), an eighteenth-century spinning wheel ($100), and a nineteenth-century still life painting of fruit ($65).

• **PENACOOK**. *Willow Hollow Shop*. Al and Nancy Schlegel. 185 South Main St. 603-753-4281. Open seven days a week, 10–6 (summers), 10–5 (winters). The Willow Hollow Shop carries a very wide selection of antiques displayed on three floors. Most categories of antiques and collectibles are represented, including paper, Americana, toys, tinware, tools, advertising, country store items, primitives, glass, china, furniture, and railroadiana. This is one of the largest shops in New Hampshire. This store does a great deal of national advertising and has a mail order antiques business. They publish twelve antiques catalogs that are updated daily and are available for $1 each. The Schlegels avoid depression glass and oak.

• **WEST NOTTINGHAM**. *The Unicorn Antique Shop*. Patricia J. Farr. Rt. 152. 603-942-7084. Open daily 9–6. The Unicorn shop carries a general line of antiques, collectibles, and memorabilia including specialties in oil lamps, rugs, and furniture. In addition to the antiques, they make custom-braided rugs. The shop specifically avoids bottles and books.

SEACOAST REGION

• **EAST KINGSTON**. *1680 House Antiques*. Evelyn Edwards. Jct. Rts. 108 and 107. Open Mar.–Dec. Sun., Mon., Wed., Fri. 12–5; other times by appointment. Evelyn Edwards carries country furniture and primitive articles. She has a good selection of a variety of antiques and collectibles. Her country furniture is of the 1800s, there is folk art, quilts, baskets, jewelry and some paper. The antiques are in original condition and retain their original paint. Some recent finds here were a dressing table c. 1810 with original paint; a tapered leg table; and a dry sink c. 1810, grained and original. Nothing in this shop is later than the 1920s and no Mission furniture.

• **EXETER**. *Herschel B. Burt. Antique Clocks.* Linden St. (1 mi. from Exeter Inn). 603-772-3598. Open Mon.–Fri. 9–5. Mr. Burt's shop is in an eighteenth-century house. It offers a selection of antique American clocks and rare books on horology. Recent offerings included an Aaron Willard tall clock, an S. Willard banjo clock, and a selection of New Hampshire tall clocks. Mr. Burt is Co-director of the Adams Brown Company (Box 399, Exeter, NH 03833) which offers by mail a selection of over 300 books on horology including some reprints of old catalogs.

Exeter Craft Center Shop. 61 Water St. 603-778-8282. Open Mon.–Sat. 9:30–5. The Exeter Crafts Center is a member of the League of New Hampshire Craftsmen. The Center, which exhibits and sells the handcrafts of New Hampshire artisans, is a nonprofit outlet for their crafts. Some of the work includes stoneware pottery, porcelain, limited production, and one-of-a-kind jewelry, metal work, wood furniture and accessories, woven goods, apparel and accessories, fiber arts, baskets, quilts, macrame, blown and stained glass, leather, clothing and much more.

October Stone Antiques. Linda J. Rogers. Jady Hill. 603-772-2024. Open daily 10–4 and by appointment. Linda Rogers handles country furniture, country store items, primitives, clocks, and lamps. She avoids flea market items, jewelry, coins, books, dolls and items made after 1900. There recently was a youth's trundle bed ($145), a Rayo lamp ($75), and a 6-ft. country pine cupboard with panelled door and one drawer ($350). The shop is in a beautiful old barn built by Linda's family in the 1850s.

• **FREMONT**. *Spaulding and Frost Company, Inc.* 100 Main St. (Rt. 107). 603-895-4590. Open daily Mar. 1–Dec. 31, 12–5. This company has been making barrels in the same location for 108 years. They are believed to be the only pine cooperage in the United States and make a variety of barrels, pails and baskets.

• **KENSINGTON**. *Kensington Historical Company.* Peter Atwood. Hickory Lane. 603-778-0686. Open by appointment only all year. The Kensington Historical Company specializes in eighteenth-century buildings and building materials. They handle architectural materials of the period and supply houses, barns, and out-buildings as well as the materials with which to restore them. Hand-hewn beams are $3.50 per lin. ft., random width flooring is $3.50 per lin. ft., and interior raised panel doors are $50.

• **NEWMARKET**. *The Mill Store*. Drake, Smith, and Company. Main St. (Rt. 108). 603-659-5443. Open Mon.–Thurs., Sat. 9–5:30; Fri. 9–8:30, Sun. 1–5:30. Drake, Smith, and Company is a major manufacturer of early-American-style furniture with more than 100 separate items in their product line. The Mill Store offers discounts of about 28 percent off retail price for first quality stock, and up to 60 percent for seconds. The company also carries Hitchcock Chair Company, Nichols and Stone Company, and other lines at 30 percent savings. Annual sales are held for five weeks beginning in January, and five weeks beginning in August. The 21,000-sq. ft. factory showroom is a small part of the factory itself which was built in 1860 on Great Bay Portsmouth Tide Head. There are salmon falls and the old salmon ladder.

• **NEWTON JUNCTION**. *Peter H. Eaton Antiques, Inc*. Thornell Rd. (4 mi. from Rt. 495—Merrimac, MA exit). 603-382-6838. Open all year every day. Peter Eaton carries only eighteenth-century American antiques and accessories. The period and country furniture is in original, as-found condition. All the merchandise is unconditionally guaranteed. There are no restored or reproduction pieces here. Mr. Eaton recently had a set of six sausage-turned ladderbacks in the original red paint, a Chippendale slant front desk in old black paint, and a set of four Windsor bow backs in old paint. The shop is located in Mr. Eaton's eighteenth-century home (with seven fireplaces!) on a lovely back road in southeastern New Hampshire.

• **PLAISTOW**. *Kay's Antique Shop*. Main St. 603-382-5305. Open Mon., Wed., Fri. 10 5, Sat. 2:30–5. Although this shop carries a general line of antiques, collectibles, and memorabilia, its specialties are small early kitchenware, pine furniture, advertising material, toys, dolls, and doll furniture. The shop does not carry large furniture. It is located in the former post office in the village. It is now a small shingled cottage.

• **PORTSMOUTH**. *Annual Street Fair*. Ceres St. 603-431-

5846. Open July. This crafts show has been an annual event for more than ten years under the sponsorship of Theatre-by-the-Sea.

Margaret Scott Carter, Inc. Hap Moore. 175 Market St. (exit 7 off I-95N, the shop is on the first block). 603-436-1781. Open Mon.–Sat. 10–5. This shop deals in antique country furniture and accessories. They specialize in decoys, antique tools, and British pewter. It is one of the largest shops in the area and contains a wide variety of unusual antiques of high quality. They do not carry any Victorian furniture or accessories. Recent finds in the shop were a primitive wheelwright's plough plane in beech, c. 1800 ($185), a handsome (9½′ × 3′) pine dining table from an English farm ($950), and a Whistler drake decoy by Gus Wilson, c. 1915 ($195). The business is housed in a restored five-story 1810 grain warehouse on the Piscataqua River.

Dexter Shoe Factory Outlet (see **Dexter, ME**). 43 Congress St.

Ore'a Designs. John Kanoules. 2859 Lafayette Rd. (Rt. 1, 3 mi. south of Portsmouth). 603-436-0264. Open all year daily 8:30–5. Ore'a Designs handcraft their own jewelry in sterling silver and 14 karat gold. They make earrings, bracelets, necklaces, chokers, collars, rings, and pins. The shop sells only its own designs.

DARTMOUTH–LAKE SUNAPEE REGION

• **CLAREMONT**. *Elderberry Antiques.* John M. Meloney. 95 Winter St. (next door to the National Guard armory, two blocks north of Rt. 103). 603-542-2111. Open all the time by chance or appointment. John Meloney carries all sorts of antiques but specializes in old tools, primitives, postcards, and oddities. He also handles old and second-hand books. The biggest following is in old wood-working, blacksmithing, tinsmithing, leather working, and related tools. He also carries some early agricultural tools, and most tools are (as much as possible) pre-Victorian. Recently Mr. Meloney had an 11-ft. auger for hand boring wooden water pipes ($65), an oval framed hand-painted photo of Lincoln ($35), an eighteenth-century dough box ($55), and a hair picker—a large hand operated machine for tangling horsehair prior to use in upholstery ($150). Military items, guns, and animal traps are specifically avoided. The shop is in a little red barn and carriage house of a Cape Cod type farmhouse built in the 1770s.

Wipco Value Centre. N. Zilch and R. C. Zilch. Newport–Claremont Rd. (Rt. 103, 6 mi. from Claremont). 603-863-1351. Open Mon.–Fri. 9:30–5, Sat. 9:30–4; extra hours in Dec. The catalog showroom has brand-name merchandise with savings of up to 50 percent. It carries a large selection of costume jewelry and gifts. Oneida Stainless Flatware (fifty-piece service for eight), regularly $76.95, is discounted here to $46.17. Seth Thomas Travel Clocks, regularly $7.95, are $4.97; American Tourister 26-inch luggage, regularly $72.50, is $46.97 here. There are many such bargains. Wipco has a winter jewelry sale the last week in December, a red-tag sale in February, and a summer clearance sale in August.

● **GUILD**. *The Dorr Mill Store*. Dorr Fabrics. Rt. 103 and Rt. 11. 603-863-1197. Open all year Mon.–Sat. 9–5. This mill outlet sells at discount prices and offers Pendleton and Dorr woolens, remnants and seconds, cottons, sewing notions and craft supplies including rug wool, kits for hooking, crewel, needlepoint, weaving, shirret, and patchwork. The store also has a supply of knitting yarns, sweaters, and blankets. The supply of remnants is continually changing as new items are brought across the street from the Dorr mill.

● **HANOVER**. *League of New Hampshire Craftsmen—Hanover Shop*. 13 Lebanon St. 603-643-5050. Open year-round Mon.–Sat. 9:30–5. This shop, like all League shops shows only the work of its members and to exhibit there, the craftsperson must submit samples of her or his work to a jury of experienced craftspeople. Virtually every sort of craft is available here, from pottery to leather, glass to metals and wood. The store is a nonprofit outlet for New Hampshire craftspeople.

Marie-Louise Antiques. Marie-Louise Fredyma. Lyme Rd. (Rt. 10). 603-643-4276. Open all year Mon.–Sat. 8:30–4:30. This shop carries china, glass, jewelry, sterling serving and flatware, furniture, pewter and copper. The china and glass are primarily Victorian, American and French. Also handled are art glass and pottery.

Recent offerings included a Staffordshire hen on a nest ($175), a stuffing spoon in Audubon by Tiffany ($150), a Shaker weaving chair with tape seat and original finish ($225) and a pewter porringer by RG ($225). Ms. Fredyma avoids depression glass, Oriental rugs, and Oriental china.

• **LEBANON**. *Sugar Hill Furniture Showroom* (outlet). (see **Lisbon, NH**). 195 Mechanic St. 603-448-3970.

• **LYME**. *Claflin House—"Antiques and Embellishments."* Constance Bergendoff. On the Common (10 mi. north of Hanover on Rt. 10). 603-795-2528. Open 9–5 and by appointment. Constance Bergendoff carries early country antiques in their original condition. Her collection, ten rooms full of antiques, is excellent and contains early country furniture, hooked rugs, samplers, quilts, and stoneware. The furniture includes cupboards, hutch tables, sets of chairs, arm chairs, blanket chests, and light tables. In addition, there are many old baskets. Recently there were forty-five samplers ($150–$1200), eight blanket chests with original decorations ($300–$950), and thirty quilts ($200–$350). The hooked rugs come in a variety of sizes from small area rugs to room sized. Claflin House avoids glass, china, Victorian items, and oak. It is located in a lovely 1850 house on the common.

• **NEW LONDON**. *The Artisan's Workshop*. Muffin Bushueff. Main St. (New London exit off I-89). 603-526-4227. Open Mon.–Sat. 10–5. Closed Tues. in winter. Artisan's Workshop exhibits and sells arts and crafts, and carries supplies and gifts as well. The shop has handcrafted jewelry, functional and decorative pottery, leather, macrame, stained glass, paintings, prints, photographs, cards, and stationery all from local artists and craftspeople. There are sterling rings ranging from $2.50 for a simple band to $12–$40 for a stone setting; wildlife prints from $3 and up; and miniature watercolors and oils by local artists, $3 and up. Among the supplies available here are: artists' materials, macrame supplies, beads and findings for jewelry, and assorted craft kits. The shop is located in an 1847 white clapboard inn on Main Street. The inn also houses Peter Christian's Tavern.

The Mad Eagle, Inc., Antiques. Colonel and Mrs. P. H. Lash. Rt. 11. 603-526-4880. Open daily May to Oct. 10–5. This shop carries a line of American period furniture and accessories that mostly predate 1840. Included are china, glass, porcelain, pewter, brass, copper, tin, clocks, Oriental rugs, frog mugs, children's name mugs, miniature chests, and spice chests. Recent offerings included a New England tiger maple highboy ($5200), advertisement pine spice chest ($210), a six-drawer bracket base chest ($3000), and a maple country Chippendale side chair ($180). The owners avoid carnival and depression glass.

• **NEWBURY**. *Annual Craft Fair*. Sunapee State Park. 603-224-3375. August. This show has been an annual event since 1934. It is sponsored by the League of New Hampshire Craftsmen, which has more than 4 thousand members. The show is juried by actual works and limited to members of the League.

• **PLAINFIELD**. *Wells Wood*. Rt. 12A. 603-675-5360. Call for shop hours. Wells Wood is a marvelous baronial estate, the former home of Maxfield Parrish. It is famed for its luxurious lodgings and food. Rosalind and Thomas Wells also maintain a shop on the grounds of the estate. From their travels, they have filled the shop with antiques, gifts, collectibles and Maxfield Parrish memorabilia. The Gallery Hall features the works of recognized local artists. Wells Wood is situated in the heart of the famous Cornish Art Colony in Plainfield. Plainfield also has its own Auction Gallery.

• **SALISBURY HEIGHTS**. *Barker's of Salisbury Heights*. Eileen and Dana Barker. Rt. 4 (opposite Town Library). 603-648-2488. Open daily all year 9–5 and evenings by appointment. The Barkers handle a general line of antiques including furniture, old tools, mirrors, and lamps. They do not carry oak, depression glass, clocks, or bottles. The shop is located in a 1795 center-chimney colonial house in a picturesque village of the same era.

• **SOUTH ACWORTH**. *Gehan Family Pottery*. Dan Gehan. Rt. 123A. 603-835-6033. Open Wed.–Sun. 11–5. This shop carries hand-made stoneware pottery, all of which is made in the studio. Their functional pottery is decorated with drawings of motifs and scenes indigenous to rural New England. The glazing is off-white with blue drawings. Some examples of their work include a medium open casserole decorated on the inside with a scene of sheep in the field ($20) and a child's bowl with a drawing of a truck inside ($12.50). The Gehans have sales on Memorial Day and Columbus Day weekends when they offer their stock at a 10 percent discount.

• **SUNAPEE**. *Priscilla Drake Antiques and Seven Hearths Country Store*. Rt. 11. 603-763-5546. Open May 1–Dec. 24, 10–5. This shop carries period furniture, largely of pine, cherry, and maple; English and American pewter, Chinese export china, brass, and glass. Recent offerings included a Maple Queen Anne drop-leaf table ($2800), a walnut Pembroke table with drawer ($850), and a large canton tureen without top ($350). The shop is in an 1801 home with wide board floors, hand-hewn beams, and a large beehive oven in the main room.

• **WARNER**. *Town Tree Antiques*. John Eastman and Peter Lovejoy. Kirtland St. (second left off Kearsarge St.). 603-456-3802. Open 10–5 " 'most every day" July and Aug.; Sept.–June, open Sat. and by chance or appointment. Town Tree handles only antiques. The shop carries country store articles, advertising, primitives, and country furniture. In addition there are postcards, ironware, paintings, early books, posters, old bottles, stoneware, and copper. Some of their recent finds include a Post Office front ($350), a railroad pot-belly stove ($250), an old blue six-board blanket chest ($85), a tin Orange Crush thermometer ($32), and a pine corner cupboard ($975).

• **WASHINGTON**. *Tintagel Antiques*. Sally Krone. Rt. 31 (1 mi. north of the village). Open 10–5 mid-May to mid-October. Closed Thurs. Mrs. Krone specializes in country antiques and primitives with special selections of woodenware, tin, cast iron, frames, copper, brass, tools, kitchenware, and small furniture pieces.

• **WENTWORTH**. *Bernier Studio*. Rt. 25. 603-764-5720. Open daily, mid-June to mid-Oct., 10–6. This store carries a variety of items, among them stained glass, made on the premises by Emery Bernier. Other crafts include pottery, wrought iron, sculpture, blown glass, woodenware, dolls and toys, jewelry, braided rugs, and candles. There is also a boutique with women's clothing, a selection of books on Americana, New England, and other subjects, and a variety of foodstuffs including pickles, jams, maple syrup, honey, and herbs. The shop is in a restored, stately colonial house.

• **WEST LEBANON**. *The Artifactory*. Gordon Thomas. Colonial Plaza (Rt. 12A). 603-298-8592. Open 10–6. Closed Mon. This is a collection of crafts and gifts representing the work of over forty-five artists from fourteen states. There is jewelry in all sorts of media including fossilized ivory and carved bone; leather purses, wallets, and belts; stained glass; pottery, both functional and decorative; woodwork, candles, macrame, photography, bronze bells and more.

LAKES REGION

• **ASHLAND**. *The Raven Antiques*. Bob and Jane Kroeger. Main St. 603-968-7675. Open 10–5 daily all year. The Kroegers carry a line of country furniture, decorative related items, and antique clothing. The offerings include country furniture and primitives, baskets, quilts, tinware, rugs, pottery, and an assortment of clothing, mostly Victorian, including whites, ladies suits, dresses, shawls, hats, furs, and other accessories. Recent offerings included a country pine cupboard with paneled door ($350), a bird cage windsor chair ($110), and a basket design quilt ($60). The shop does not carry much glass or fine china.

• **CENTER SANDWICH**. *Ayottes' Designery*. Robert and Roberta Ayotte. Rt. 113. 603-284-6915. Open 10–5. Closed Sun. and Wed. Robert and Roberta graduated from Rhode Island School of Design in Providence in 1958 and have been full-time designers and weavers of woolen fabrics and wall hangings since 1966. The Designery is located in an old rambling building that was formerly the local high school and dates to 1856. The Ayottes now weave a broad line of fabrics which are fashioned into an exclusive line of apparel including capes, coats, dresses, gowns, skirts, jumpers, tunics, etc. They also make ready-made and made to order wall hangings.

● **LACONIA**. *Dexter Shoe Factory Outlet* (see **Dexter, ME**). 369 Union Ave.

● **MERIDETH**. *Burlwood Antique Shop and Market*. Thomas and Nancy Lindsey. U.S. Rt. 3. 603-279-6387. The shop is open daily April 1–Christmas, 10–4. The Market is open every Fri., Sat., and Sun. June–Labor Day, 10–6; Sat. and Sun. June 1–Oct. 12, 10–6. The Lindseys' shop handles only antiques with a general line that includes furniture from the eighteenth century (American) through Victorian oak, early Staffordshire chinas, soft paste and flow blue, coin and sterling silver flatware, jewelry, paintings, prints, antique tools, and primitives. Recent offerings included a whale oil lantern with original burner ($115), an American birch and maple Hepplewhite tall clock ($1800), and a flow blue "Scinde" 10-inch plate ($40). In addition to the shop, the Lindseys have converted a large lodge and outbuilding into a summer and fall antique market which has thirty to thirty-five antique dealers in attendance. The Lindseys try to maintain an "antiques only" policy so that the atmosphere is antiques mart rather than flea market.

Merideth-Laconia Arts and Crafts. Rt. 3. 603-279-7920. Open May–Dec., daily 9:30–5:30 except Thanksgiving and Christmas. This shop is a member of the League of New Hampshire Craftsmen, hence the craftspeople represented have been chosen by juries of highly competent League craftspeople. Included in the shop's offerings are functional and decorative pottery, weaving, spinning, fiber arts, graphics, enamelware, stoneware, jewelry, leather, macrame, knitting, woodworking, stained glass, metalwork, quilts, blown glass, pressed flowers, and cut and pierced lampshades.

● **OSSIPEE**. *Hoopers Farm Antique Shop*. Ed and Eleanor Hooper. Rt. 16 (turn south at jct. Rts. 28 and 16). 603-539-6834. Open year-round by chance or appointment. The Hoopers carry a general line of antiques and collectibles. The shop features folk art, Sandwich glass, American Indian items, early photographs and primitives. This is good New Hampshire barn antiquing. In addition to the above, the Hoopers have early clothing, paper, books, furniture, sterling, miniatures, sheet music, advertising, White Mountain Art, and Shaker items. The shop recently had a Shaker

A classic New England interior *(The Vermont Country Store, Inc., Weston, VT)*

Antique andirons and early implements (*Hardings of Hancock, Hancock, NH*)

Sewing or cheese basket patterned with hexagons (*Wheat and Chaff Antiques, Hopkinton, NH*)

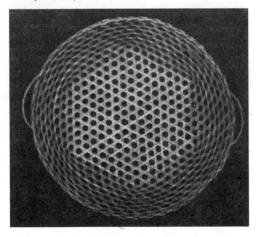

The Pandora Factory Store, Manchester, NH

Wooden truck with cargo *(Kee Pon Truckin' Co., Milford, NH)*

Dealer's booth *(Burlwood Antique Shop and Market, Meredith, NH)*

Beech wheelwright's plow plane, ca. 1800 *(Margaret S. Carter, Inc., Portsmouth, NH)*

An antique toaster, a sea captain's wooden leg, a ladder-back chair, and three pieces of early wooden ware *(Burlwood Antique Shop and Market, Meredith, NH)*

Eighteenth-century American antiques *(Peter H. Eaton Antiques, Inc., Newton Junction, NH)*

A picturesque board game first sold in 1898 *(The Game Preserve, Peterborough, NH)*

Baskets galore *(Basketville Store, Putney, VT)*

Decorative glass shade *(The Artifactory, West Lebanon, NH)*

Hand-wrought jewelry *(The Artifactory, West Lebanon, NH)*

Chasing in reeding on a piece of seventeenth-century silver *(Thompsons Studio, Inc., Damariscotta, ME)*

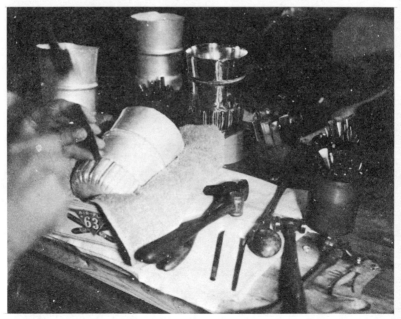

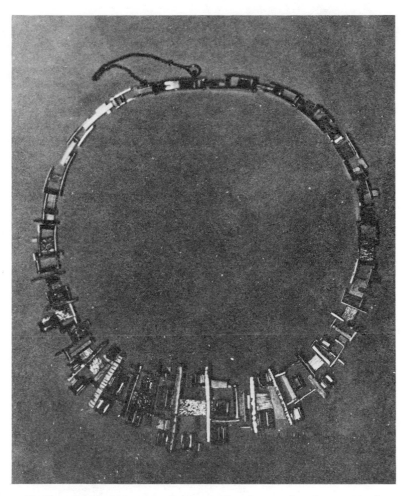

Necklace fashioned of green and yellow gold with tourmaline that was mined in Maine *(Thompsons Studio, Inc., Damariscotta, ME)*

Ornamental box *(Calista Sterling Antiques, Ellsworth, ME)*

Flow blue china *(Donald and Lois Tucker Antiques, North Berwick, ME)*

Stained glass *(No Trumpets—No Drums, Ogunquit, ME)*

Wooden table with candlestick, teapot, andirons, and fire screen *(The Captain's House, Searsport, ME)*

Decorated stoneware *(Keag River Pottery, South Thomaston, ME)*

Ornate antique parlor heater with brass accessories *(Bryant Steel Works, Thorndike, ME)*

candle dryer, an American Indian horsehair and porcupine hair adornment called a roach, and an eighteenth-century tall wig stand with original decorations. The shop is in the Hooper house and barn which were built in the early 1800s. The shop is in the old barn with hand-hewn beams and wooden peg construction.

• **ROCHESTER**. *Strafford Corner Antiques*. Peter Carswell. 293 Pond Hill Rd. 603-332-4264. Open by chance or by appointment. The Strafford Corner carries a general line mostly purchased from local sources with the emphasis on country furniture and accessories including clocks, paintings, and folk art. Recent offerings included a pair of country paintings of a cat and a dog, c. 1840; a refinished tavern table; an upright cobbler's bench with its old paint; and a weight-driven schoolhouse clock (D. Pratt's Son, Maker). This shop avoids art and pressed glass. It is located on a restored country farm.

• **RUMNEY**. *Mill Road Antiques*. The Munkittricks. Mill Rd. 603-786-2101. Open all year: winter months by chance or appointment; other seasons 10–5 daily. The Munkittricks' line includes flow blue china, early marked Bennington in Rockingham, Flint enamel and porcelain glaze, and rare decorated stoneware. Recent offerings included a Ben Franklin pitcher, marked 1849, Bennington ($300) and a decorated stoneware churn, Julius Norton, Bennington, 1841–1845 ($195).

• **SANBORNVILLE**. *Aladdin Antiques*. Liz Olimpio. Governor's Rd. (½ mi. west off Rt. 16). 603-522-8503. Open daily 10–6, and by appointment. Aladdin's specializes in toys, old banks, and dolls. There are also primitives and "oddball items" but the emphasis is on children's things, dollhouse articles, and mechanical and still banks. Liz Olimpio does not carry Oriental antiques. She recently has had a large colored Lithopane lamp with many colored scenes ($800), an A.M. bisque head doll with kid body, 22 in. high ($125) and a mechanical bank with a monkey and coconuts ($450). The shop section of the natural shingled building has a beautiful stained-glass door from an old church.

• **SOUTH WOLFEBORO**. *The Schoolhouse Shop*. 603-569-3489. Open May–Dec. daily 9–5. This shop is a member of the League of New Hampshire Craftsmen and offers a wide selection of local crafts including batik, clothing, dolls, glass, jewelry, leather, needlework, functional and decorative pottery, quilts, soft sculpture, tole painting, wall hangings, weavings, woodcraft, blown glass, and macrame. The building is an old two-room schoolhouse whose bell still rings.

Touchmark Antiques. Anne Roome and Helen Bradley. Rt. 28 (across from the Baptist Church). 603-569-2572. Open May–Oct. daily and by appointment anytime. Touchmark features primitive and country furniture (small pieces), antique kitchen equipment and decorative furnishings. They have woodenware of all sorts, baskets, sleds, antique metals, old tools and some antique clothing. There are polished copper boilers ($40–$60), a refinished wagon seat ($75) and a child's sled with original stencil, in good condition ($55). The shop does not handle jewelry, clocks, silver, or crystal.

● **TAMWORTH**. *The Slop Chest Antiques*. Ralph Raabe. Rt. 16. 603-367-4715. Open 10–5 daily all year. This shop carries a general line of antiques which includes period furniture, tall case clocks, Regulator clocks, period copper and brass, some nautical items, and lamps. Mr. Raabe avoids depression and carnival glass, coins, stamps, and jewelry. The shop is on an L-shaped veranda that is part of an early nineteenth-century white clapboard building.

● **WEIRS BEACH**. *Craftsmen's Fairs and Flea Markets*. Various weekends Memorial Day–Labor Day, 9–4. These events are held frequently all summer. For details, contact the Lakes Region Association, P.O. Box 30, Wolfeboro, NH 03894 (phone 603-569-1117).

● **WOLFEBORO**. *Annual Antiques Show*. Kingswood Regional High School. Mid-August. Fifty antique dealers display their wares at this annual event, which is now in its twenty-fifth year. Admission is $1.50.

WHITE MOUNTAINS REGION

● **CHOCORUA**. *Chocorua Potters. Bob and Jane Solar*. Rt.

16. 603-323-7939. Open summer 10–6 daily, winter 10–5 daily except Wed. Chocorua Potters is a potter's studio and display gallery, housed in an 1840s barn. Stoneware and porcelain, traditional and contemporary, functional and display pieces are available. The shop also sells pre-mixed clay.

• **CONWAY.** *Dexter Shoe Factory Outlet* (see **Dexter, ME**). Rt. 16.

Pine Crafters of New Hampshire, Inc. Kancamagus Hwy. (Rt. 112). 603-447-2150. Open Mon.–Fri. May 15–Oct. 30, 9:30–5. Pine Crafters limits its factory output to a line of pine tables that includes two end tables, a coffee table, a studio table, three game tables, and a dining table. Custom-made tables are also available. All tables are made with 2-in. thick pine tops (one piece except for the dining tables which use two matched pieces) and all are finished in alcohol resistant finishes. Unfinished tables are available at lower prices.

White Mountain Woolens, Inc. Rt. 16. 603-447-2443. Open in winter Mon.–Sat. 10 5:30, Sun. 12–5; summer Mon.–Sat. 9–9, Sun. 9–5:30. White Mountain Woolens specializes in wool fabrics and yarns. The shop also carries a complete line of cotton fabrics, patterns, and accessories, as well as all forms of needlecrafts and supplies and rug hooking and braiding supplies. It is a direct mill outlet for several mills and carries a full line of New England woolens from $3.50 up. The shop has an annual sale each February during Washington's Birthday week.

• **FRANCONIA.** *Franconia Arts and Crafts Shop.* Glaessel Building near Tramway. Open daily 9–5, May–Oct. Franconia Arts and Crafts Shop is owned by the nonprofit League of New Hampshire Craftsmen, which exhibits and sells the work of area craftspeople. Featured in the shop are earthenware, stoneware, porcelain, jewelry, metal holloware, wooden furniture and accessories, weavings, quilts, macrame, blown and stained glass, enamels, leather, clothing, decoupage, toys, and candles.

• **FRANKLIN.** *The Hosiery Mill Store.* Cormier Hosiery Mill. Central St. 603-934-5452. Open all year Mon.–Fri. 9–5, Sat. 9–4. This mill outlet sells hosiery for the entire family, body suits, warm up suits, terry slippers, and knit material. Some sample prices include terry slippers for $1.39, warm-up suits (irregular) $15, body suits (irregular) $2.75, and knit material (mostly 60 in. wide) $1.50 per yard.

- **JACKSON**. *Wildcat Valley Country Store*. Elishu Perkins. Jct. Rt. 16A and Jackson Village Rd. 603-383-9612. Open daily June–Jan. 10–6; Jan.–June weekends 11–5. The building in which this store is housed was built in 1846 as a blacksmith shop and has served as a country store for more than 50 years. The store retains its antique fixtures and has an old coffee roaster. Selections include staple and fancy dry goods, imported teas and coffees, cheddar cheese, crackers from the barrel, jams, jellies, and smoked pudding. There are candles, books, toys, soaps, and a large selection of gifts. Also in stock is a selection of kitchen tools, woodenware, herbs and botanicals.

- **LINCOLN**. *Loon Mountain Arts and Crafts Festival*. Loon Mountain. 603-745-8111. This arts and crafts show is held annually in August. It is an open show.

  Loon Mountain Indian Powwow. Kancamagus Hwy. (Rt. 112) 603-745-8111. Late July. This annual event brings together native Americans from many nations across the country and features arts and crafts sales, dancing, food, and various Indian ceremonies.

- **LISBON**. *Sugar Hill Furniture Showroom*. 95 Main St. (Rt. 302). 603-838-6677. Open Mon.–Sat. 9:30–5:30, spring–fall Sun. 9–5:30. This is a factory outlet for Sugar Hill furniture. A wide variety of gifts and accessories are also sold here. The store features 30 percent discounts on all furniture. The second floor has huge discounts of up to 70 percent off retail price on returned, discontinued, or slightly damaged items. Sugar Hill has three big sales—Last Leaf Sale in the fall, First Flower Sale in spring, and Red Dot Sale in the winter.

- **LITTLETON**. *Annual Sidewalk Art and Craft Show*. Last Sat. in Sept. This annual event attracts almost a hundred artists and craftspeople from the Northeast. In addition to these exhibits, the Rotary Club sponsors a Lobster and Clambake Festival for the benefit of the local hospital during the time of this show. For further information call the Chamber of Commerce at 603-444-2351.

Brookside Antiques. A. M. Wright. Bethlehem Rd. (Rt. 302). 603-444-2986. Open daily 9–5. This shop has a diversified line including china, glass, household furnishings, and accessories.

The Cupola. Marjorie Durdle. 187 Main St. 603-444-5780. Open June–Oct. 10–5 daily. This shop is located in the center of town at the rear of the Littleton Motel. The shop carries a general line of antiques, collectibles, and gifts that stresses country furniture, primitives, and glass china. The Cupola specifically avoids stamps, postcards, and bottles. The barn in which The Cupola is located was built in 1840–1850 as a stable for a large townhouse.

● **NORTH CONWAY**. *Eastern Mountain Sports, Inc.* Eastern Slope Inn. 603-356-5433. Open daily 9–9; during the off season (Labor Day–Thanksgiving and March 1–Memorial Day) Mon.–Thurs. 9–6. Eastern Mountain Sports is one of the nation's leading suppliers of hiking and mountaineering supplies including down and other jackets, backpackets, sleeping bags, packs and pack frames, boots, camping equipment, climbing equipment, skis, tents, and books on hiking and mountaineering. The company, which has a number of retail outlets throughout the country, offers cross-country skiing lessons, mountaineering and ice climbing instruction, and much more. This particular outlet is in a complex of stores that includes the Great Eastern restaurant, business offices, a garden shop, tennis and swimming club, and the EMS Lodge, next door.

Kittery Mills of North Conway, Inc. Kearsarge St. (off Rts. 16 and 302). 603-356-5438. Open winter: daily 10–6, Fri. until 9 P.M.; Summer: Mon.–Sat. 10–9, Sun. 10–6. Kittery Mills sells designer sportswear for men and women at 40 percent or more off retail prices. Some of the brand names are Jones, New York, Diane von Furstenberg, Pierre Cardin, Ralph Lauren, Christian Dior, and many more.

The Log Cabin—Antiques. Richard M. Plusch. Main St. (on Rts. 16 and 302). Shop: 603-356-3333; home: 603-383-9222. Open in winter Sat. and Sun. 10–5; summer daily 10–5 and by appointment. Log Cabin Antiques handles American country furniture and fine glass such as blown, Flint, pattern, and cut. The furniture and glass are mostly eighteenth- and early nineteenth-century, but there is a large inventory of other antiques of quality. Richard Plusch had a Queen Anne Chest on Chest in excellent condition for $5500; a painted table (as seen in *American Painted Furniture 1660–1880* by Dean Fales, Jr. Plate 495, p. 275) for $850; and a pair of deep sapphire blue Sandwich candlesticks (as seen in *McKearin* plate 200, #29) for $600 a pair. The shop is a nineteenth-century log cabin.

● **NORTH HAVERHILL**. *Marjorie Barry*. Rt. 116 (½ mi. from Rt. 10). 603-787-6212. Open May–Oct. by chance or appointment. Marjorie Barry offers an ever-changing stock of antiques, collectibles, and memorabilia. Her stock includes refinished country furniture (pine, oak, etc.), pattern glass, hand-painted china, sterling silver, Victorian jewelry, primitives and children's items. Recently there was an unusual brass match holder with a vulture in great detail ($65) and a five-piece blue Bohemian dresser set ($85). The shop is located in a new split-level home in a picturesque country setting.

● **WEST CAMPTON**. *New Hampshire Homecraft Shop*. Rt. 3 (south of the village). 603-726-8626. Open daily, mid-June to mid-Oct. 9:30–5. This shop is a cooperative that was founded in 1961 and limits itself to the sale of members' craft works. All crafts are made by New Hampshire residents, and offerings include rugs, woodwork, pickles, aprons, notepaper, pillows, crochet, afghans, clothing, paintings, jams and jellies, jewelry, sneakers, mittens, pillowcases, knitting, ceramics, wood carving, dolls, and toys.

Maine

VISITORS WILL FIND the vast state of Maine to be a shoppers' delight. Crafts lovers should be particularly pleased with the offerings in this state. There are more than 1300 members of the six crafts organizations in this state.

Before leaving on your trip to Maine, we suggest that you write for helpful travel information from the Maine Publicity Bureau (a private organization) and the state Chamber of Commerce and Department of Commerce and Industry. Their addresses are: Maine Publicity Bureau, 922 Gateway Circle, Portland, ME 04102; Maine State Chamber of Commerce, 477 Congress St., Portland, ME 04111; and Maine Department of Commerce and Industry, State House, Augusta, Maine 04330.

The listings of shops that follows is grouped into three sections by geographical location: the South Coast (south of Thomaston) includes coastal and near-coastal towns; the North Coast (north of Thomaston); and Inland Maine. Within each section, the towns are listed alphabetically.

SOUTH COAST (south of Thomaston)

• **ARUNDEL**. *Especially Maine*. Katherine M. Pulkkinen. Jct. Vinegar Hill Rd. and Rt. 1. 207-985-3749. Open all year Mon.–Sat. 9:30–5. Especially Maine carries mostly Maine products (98 percent) with a few notable exceptions. All items purchased

MAINE

Scale of miles
0   20   40   60

Map by Jaber

Primary roads

Secondary roads

here, either at the store or through the mail order business, are guaranteed to be 100 percent satisfactory or you may receive your money back or have the item replaced. The Shop features fine handcrafts, gourmet food, clothing made in Maine, books, and furniture. The locally made chamois cloth skirts are perhaps the most famous of all their items.

• **BATH**. *Yankee Artisan*. Ruth Jacob. 119 Front St. (along the waterfront). 207-443-6215. Open Mon.–Sat. 9–5. Yankee Artisan is a craft cooperative featuring the work of Maine craftspeople in the following media: pottery, weaving, graphics, painting, jewelry, leather, macrame, knitting, and woodworking, carving, and quilting. The shop is located in the historic downtown Bath district along the Kennebec River. The shop has nice oak paneling and a fireplace.

• **BOOTHBAY HARBOR**. *Dexter Shoe Factory Outlet*. (see **Dexter**). Boothbay Harbor Shopping Center.

• **BRUNSWICK**. *Dexter Factory Shoe Outlet* (see **Dexter**). 106 Pleasant St.

• **CAPE ELIZABETH**. *Pillsbury's Antiques*. Mary Alice Pillsbury. Two Lights Rd. 207-799-0638. Open May–Oct. but call in advance to be sure. This shop carries antiques, collectibles, and herbs. The emphasis is on pine and oak furniture, primitives, brass and copper, glass, china, accessories, kitchen utensils, tools, and clocks. The shop is in a barn attached to the Pillsbury's antique Cape style home.

• **CHERRYFIELD**. *Ricker Blacksmith Shop*. Main St. 207-546-7954. Open year-round Mon.–Fri. 8–5, Sat. 8–12. This shop offers functional wrought iron, custom work and authentic reproductions of colonial and nineteenth-century items. Some specialties include fireplace tools, andirons, and marine items. Visitors are welcome to watch the smith at the forge. Some examples of their work include stove pokers ($8), andirons ($40 and up), door knockers ($20) and reproduction trivets ($7.50).

• **CUMBERLAND CENTER**. *United Maine Craftsmen Fair*. Cumberland Fairgrounds. Blanchard Rd. (between the two I-95s). 207-666-3447. Open middle weekend in Aug., Fri. and Sat. 10–8, Sun. 10–5.

This Fair is sponsored by the United Maine Craftsmen, who

represent a thousand people. The show features 250 craftspeople exhibiting works ranging from nostalgic traditionalism to contemporary design. Besides the exhibits visitors may shop at an old fashioned country store and feast on nature foods at the various booths. Admission: $1 adults; children under 12 free; senior citizens 50¢.

● **DAMARISCOTTA.** *The Ditty Box Antiques.* George and Muriel Lewis. Rt. 1 (adjacent to Clarissa Illsley Tavern). 207-644-8390. Open mid-June–mid-September Mon.–Sat. 10–5, Sun. 12–5. The Lewises specialize in an extensive line of Royal Doulton china but their general line includes country furniture, folk art and eighteenth- and nineteenth-century Staffordshire pottery.

Thompsons Studio, Inc. Ernest and Evelyn Thompson, Jr. and Heather and Clayton. Back Meadow Rd. (call for directions). 207-563-5280. Open all year Mon.–Sat. 10–5, and by appointment. The Thompsons have a family studio involving Ernest and Evelyn and their children, Heather and Clayton. They create and restore sterling holloware and gold and silver jewelry in the traditions of the early silversmiths. The entire family is wonderfully creative and produces heirlooms of impeccable quality. The family designs items to order in a wide variety of articles and styles: fine diamond jewelry, a detailed miniature of Revere's Silver, an elaborate English Elizabethan Wine Cup, replicas of seventeenth-century Colonial American Silver, or a modern tea set or contemporary chalice. At the time of this printing they were working on items commemorating an 850th anniversary of a castle in Wales. The Thompsons also restore and repair silver holloware and design items to replace missing companion pieces.

The Victorian Stable. Mr. and Mrs. Milton H. Plummer. Water St. (one block off Main St.). 207-563-3810. Open 10–5 daily June 1–Oct. 1 and by appointment. The Victorian Stable is an original stable which retains the box stalls faced with black walnut and topped with wrought-iron grillwork. The shop, which was built by a shipbuilder during the clipper ship days, carries the work of over 100 Maine arts and crafts people exclusively. All crafts media (except plastics) are available here from the artists, among them

Goodrich enamels, Priscilla batiks, Effie Lewis papier mache, and Robert Bartlett glass.

● **EAST BOOTHBAY**. *Andersen Studio*. Weston and Brenda Andersen. Andersen Rd. 207-633-4397. Open Mon.–Fri. 8–4:30, Sat. and Sun. 9–5. The Andersen Studio produces hand-cast stoneware in which individual pieces are produced from the original molds of Mr. and Mrs. Andersen. Each of the pieces is cast, fettled, and decorated by a single craftsman who is assigned to that piece; therefore, there are inherent minute differences among the finished pieces. This form of individualized production pottery is relatively unusual for this sort of artistic product. Most of the pieces produced by the Andersens and their assistants are animals and include penguins, seagulls, squirrels, owls, seals, ducks, and pelicans.

● **FREEPORT**. *L. L. Bean's*. Main St. 207-865-3111. Open 24 hours a day every day of the year. L. L. Bean's is a New England institution. Best known for its catalog that is mailed out by the many thousands each year, the company headquarters are always open and the showroom facilities were greatly enlarged and (not too alarmingly) modernized a few years back. Here the shopper will find something for almost everyone, with the emphasis on items for the outdoors. There are shirts, shoes, boots (including Mr. Bean's famous hunting boot, first developed in 1912), fly rods and flies, binoculars, cameras, knapsacks and picnic baskets, Hudson Bay Blankets, snowshoes, furniture, camping supplies, dried foods (for backpackers), a large selection of books, canoes, knives, traps, saws and axes, compasses, sleeping bags, tents, down and other coats, and more, and more, and more. The store also rents and sells cross-country skiing supplies in the winter months. This is a fine southern Maine stop, no matter what your final destination.

Goldsmithing by Steve and Judy Brown. 1 Mechanic St. (near L. L. Bean's). 207-865-6263. Open year-round Tues.–Sat. 11–5. The Browns make hand-crafted, original design jewelry in sterling, 14-karat gold (yellow and white), and some 18-karat gold. They use precious stones such as diamonds, rubies, sapphires, emeralds, and opals as well as semiprecious stones. Hand-crafted wedding and engagement rings are their specialties. They make a pair of 14-karat yellow gold wedding bands, octagonal in shape ($250) and a hand-carved (flower motif) and antiqued engagement and wedding-ring set with a .34 karat diamond in the engagement ring ($660). They carry a popular line of sterling silver earrings for pierced ears, including an oval pair ($14). Their shop is in a 103-year-old Masonic Hall which they have restored.

William M. Wasson, Blacksmith. Lower Main St. 207-865-3602. Open Mon.–Sat. 10–5 June–Aug., and 10–9 from Sept. to May. Mr. Wasson makes shop signs, decorative iron, iron and wood items, weathervanes, and other blacksmith items.

● **KENNEBUNK**. *Dexter Shoe Factory Outlet* (see **Dexter**). Shopper's Village.

Savon Shoes. Rt. 1. 207-985-4461. Open in summer Tues., Wed., Sat. 9–5; Mon., Thurs., Fri. 9–8. Winter Mon.–Sat. 9–5. Savon carries a complete selection of better grade and name brand shoes and handbags with an emphasis on Bally of Switzerland (20 to 60 percent off list) as well as Rosina, Ferrigamo, Schiavone, Mikelos, Selby, Cobblers, and Famolare, all at 15 to 25 percent off. Susan Gail Handbags are 20 percent off. Special sales are held around January 1 and August 1.

● **KENNEBUNKPORT**. *The Chapman House*. Louise and Thomas Chapman. Beach St. 207-967-3005. Open 9–9 daily all year, in winter by chance or appointment. The Chapmans specialize in country furniture and accessories, including fireplace equipment, brass and iron accessories, some paintings, boxes, and chests. Wall cabinets made from old walnut frames are also available made to order. Recent offerings included an empire secretary, c. 1820, in birch and pine ($650); a New Hampshire dry sink ($475); a primitive hooded cradle ($225), and a set of four pillow-back Hitchcock chairs with rush seats ($350). The Chapmans avoid oak furniture. The shop is a barn-workshop built in 1849 by a spar maker. The original workbench runs the entire length of the building on the second floor.

Golden Whale. Mary Fisher. Wharf Lane. 207-967-3151. Open June 15–Sept. 15, 10–5. Mary Fisher's shop is in an old, weathered, shingled building on the Kennebunk River. The shop was formerly a boat repair shop. She carries antiques and collectibles including porcelain, toys, brass, copper, tin, fabrics, and miniatures. The Golden Whale specifically avoids Victorian items.

Old Fort Shoppe and Gallery. Marjorie Brass. Old Fort Ave. 207-967-2709. Open May–Nov. 10–6; Nov.–May by appointment. This shop carries antiques, collectibles, and memorabilia with the emphasis on paintings, prints, primitives, jewelry, china, glass, toys, books, Oriental rugs, Oriental china, fine needlework, and eighteenth- and nineteenth-century furniture. Recent offerings included an eighteenth-century maple Chippendale desk, a Sheraton drop-front desk, a Civil War painting, and a collection of Oriental porcelains. The shop is in the former carriage house of the Old Fort Inn which was built in 1880. The Brasses also operate the Old Fort Club (luxury apartments for summer rental) on the same site.

The Sea Crafters. Ness and Bill Berey. Ocean Ave. (at the head of Old Walker's Wharf). 207-967-2059. Open May–Dec. 9:30–5:30. Closed Sun. The Sea Crafters is a nautical gift shop with all manner of decorative and useful articles pertaining to the sea. The building itself is very interesting; a 1785 ship chandler's shop constructed of hand-hewn posts and beams, pit sawn wide boards, and wood pegged fastenings.

The Stones Antiques. Honey Lou and Edward Stone. Maine St. 207-967-5916. Open all year 10–5:30. The Stones limit their stock to eighteenth- and nineteenth-century furniture, china, and paintings. The antiques carried are limited to formal and high country style. Recent offerings included an eighteenth-century tilt-top lamp stand in cherry with a one-board top ($475), an American impressionist oil on canvas ($1500), and a pair of French garnitures, hand painted, c. 1810 ($350). The shop is part of a large Victorian home which is also their residence.

- **KITTERY.** *Kittery Mills, Inc.* Kittery Mini-Mall. 207-439-4258. Open summer: Mon.–Fri. 10–8, weekends 10–6; winter: daily 10–5:30, Fri. 10–8. This outlet sells men's and women's designer clothing at 40 percent or more off retail prices. Designers represented include Jones, N.Y., Diane von Furstenberg, Pierre Cardin, Ralph Lauren, Christian Dior, and more.

Seaboard Gallery Antiques. Thomas L. Hinkle. Post Rd. Associates, Rt. 1 (exit 3A from Rt. I-95, 1¾ mi. north on Rt. 1). 207-646-5335. Open in winter Wed.–Sun. 10–5; summer daily 10–5; other times by appointment. Mr. Hinkle carries country furniture of the eighteenth and nineteenth centuries, paintings and prints, ceramics and glass, and marine antiques and paintings. He specializes in old signs, and recently featured an early garage sign.

● **OGUNQUIT**. *Kittery Mills of Ogunquit, Inc.* Beach St. (off Rt. 1). 207-646-9550. Open mid-May through mid-October daily 9–9. This outlet carries men's and women's designer clothing at 40 percent or more off list. Designers handled include Jones, N.Y., Diane von Furstenberg, Pierre Cardin, Ralph Lauren, Christian Dior, and many more.

Maple Hill Pottery Craft Gallery. Nancy M. Lee. Perkins Cove. 207-644-2134. Open June 15–Labor Day, daily 10–10 P.M. The Gallery exhibits and sells quality crafts with an emphasis on functional pottery, creative fiber, imported baskets, and a variety of original jewelry. There are four special shows throughout the year featuring significant American craftspeople. In addition to the above-mentioned crafts, the shop also carries blown glass, wood bowls made from burls, soft sculpture, woven pillows, and quilts. Ms. Lee has two sales each year—one in early June and the other in late August.

No Trumpets—No Drums. Paul W. Hagen. Perkins Cove. 207-646-5161 or 207-646-7437. Open daily May 15–Oct. 15, 10–5. This shop features a variety of hand crafts including pottery (especially the production of the owner's shop—Perkins Cove Pottery), one-of-a-kind blown art glass, limited edition stained glass, silver and gold jewelry, and leatherwork. The shop is one of the oldest buildings in Perkins Cove and was restored by Mr. Hagen.

● **PORTLAND**. *Annual Maine Antique Dealers Association Shows*. Elks Club. 1945 Congress St. Open mid-March and mid-September, Tues. 12–9, Thurs. 12–6. These two shows have been held for more than fifty years under the association's sponsorship. Admission is $1.25, but discount tickets (available at member shops) and discount advertising coupons reduce admission to $1. Write the Maine Antique Dealers Association, c/o Bill Howells, 21 Pearl St., Belfast, ME 04915. Enclose a stamped, self-addressed long envelope for a list of members of the association and the exact dates of the two shows.

Dexter Shoe Factory Outlet (see **Dexter**). 334 Forest Ave.

The Marketplace, Inc. (in The Old Port Exchange). Ellen M. Higgins. 107 Exchange St. (exit 7 off I-295). 207-774-1376. Open Mon.–Sat. 10–5, Thurs. 10–8. Closed Mon. in winter. The Marketplace carries all media of fine crafts, toys, miniatures, clothes, and antiques. They feature functional pottery, blown glass, metal work, jewelry, and soft sculpture all made by Maine craftspeople. Ellen Higgins has two sales—one in January and the other in August. The shop is located in the Old Port Exchange in a wonderful old building of the Federalist period (1867).

Pat Foley's Contemporary Fibre Design. 31½ Exchange St. (Old Port Exchange area, off Congress St.). 207-772-0286. Open all year Tues.–Sat. 10–5; winter 10–4. Pat Foley's own work in fiber art which is offered here, is also available at many galleries, art dealers, and fine shops nationally. In addition to Pat's artwork, the shop carries one-of-a-kind fiber art by several other artists; also featured are sweaters—all in the shop's wools—knit to order. The shop carries an extensive line of yarns with an emphasis on fine and unusual materials from all over the world. They have a large number of weaving accessories such as beads, mill ends, feathers (no wild or endangered birds!) and more. The *Old Port Exchange* area, where the shop is located, is a restoration-reclamation project.

Spencer Candle Factory, Inc. 446 Fore St. (in the Old Port Exchange). 207-773-0552. Open all year daily 8–5. In the 1960s, the W. Spencer Company began purchasing the first of many buildings in the Old Port Exchange and thus began the restoration and reclamation of the historic old district. The Candle Factory is located in their ancient warehouse. Here they sell many varieties of candles and candle supplies. Visitors may watch the candlemakers pour and decorate the candles. Factory tours are free and include the option of dipping one's own candle (a small fee is charged for dipping).

● **SACO**. *Dexter Shoe Factory Outlet* (see **Dexter**). Portland Rd., Rt. 1.

● **WARREN**. *At the Sign of the Daisy*. Mary and Bob Helfrich. Rt. 1. 207-273-2230. Open Apr. 1–Oct. 31 Wed.–Mon. 10–5; Nov. 1–Mar. 31 by chance or appointment. The Helfrichs carry a general line that includes a wide selection of pine furniture plus country accessories, bottles, depression glass and baskets, as well as a smattering of china and pattern glass, tin, and advertising items. Recent offerings included an eighteenth-century flax wheel ($225), a refinished pine jelly cupboard ($275), a crock with blue slip flowers ($50), and a Craft Ale sign ($10). They always have a large selection of items ranging from $10 to $400. Their farmhouse was built in 1803 and is an off-white, late Federal, center-chimney building. The shop itself is a huge old barn (one of the largest still standing in Warren). As an extra bonus, visitors to the shop may go to the barnyard next to the shop and watch the antics of the farm animals which usually include sheep, a steer, rabbits, and geese.

● **WELLS**. *Dexter Shoe Factory Outlet* (see **Dexter**). Well's Corner (Rt. 1).

Hathaway Shirts Factory Outlet (see **Waterville**).

● **WESTBROOK**. *Randall L. Meyer*. 1399 Bridgton Rd. (Rt. 302). 207-854-8008. Open Mon.–Fri. 8–5, Sat. 9–4. Mr. Meyer has a diversified line of antiques including furniture, sterling silver, cut glass, antique dolls, lamps, candlesticks, pottery, books, china, paintings, clocks, miniature furniture, and pewter. The emphasis is on early American period furniture. Recent offerings included an antique mahogany, bow front, Hepplewhite style bureau, with original brass ($950); a matching pair of early Satsuma vases, 23 in., mint condition ($2200); and a very early pine tapered-leg Tavern Table, one board top, 31 in. wide ($750).

● **YARMOUTH**. *Howard Leather Store*. H. I. Small. U.S. Rt. 1. 207-846-5912. Open Mon.–Sat. 9:30–5:30, Sun. 1–5. Howard's has a large selection of leather or suede wearing apparel, handbags, and boots. Typical of savings would be a $225 leather coat marked at $150–$170. The store also carries a large selection of riding clothes, and claims to be the "first Western store east of the Mississippi." The owner is known nationwide for his down-east philosophy and is an author and self-taught artist. He gained fame as the originator of the sport of pony harness racing and as a trainer of performing horses.

Clam Festival Crafts Fair. Rowe School. 207-833-5502. Open for three days in mid-July. This annual event is held as part of the Yarmouth Clam Festival and is sponsored by the Society of Southern Maine Craftsmen.

The Pottery Shop. Peg and Dick Miller. 7 Smith St. (just off Rt. 88, near Yarmouth Boatyard). 207-846-4981. Open daily 9–5 and evenings by appointment. The Millers make functional and decorative pottery in a variety of styles. Pottery is wheel-thrown or hand-built on the premises and gas reduction–fired in their catenary arch kiln. Their stock includes weedpots, casseroles, pitchers, mugs, vases, planters, bowls, beanpots, and floor pots. Typical prices are $30 for a 2-quart casserole, $4 for a 10-oz. coffee mug, and $15 for a 2½-quart pitcher.

W. M. Schwind, Jr., Antiques. 17 East Main St. (Rt. 88). 207-846-9458. Open all year by chance or appointment; June–Oct. 15 daily 10–5. Mr. Schwind limits his stock to classic antiques, period furniture, paintings, and accessories. His shop is most representative of eighteenth- and early nineteenth-century decorative arts with the emphasis on New England items. The accessories include China Trade porcelain, prints, some toys and dollhouses, soft paste china, hooked and Oriental rugs, and clocks. Recent offerings included a Hepplewhite serpentine front card table ($950), flint glass milk pitcher in ribbed, bellflower pattern ($275), and a Queen Anne mirror, c. 1730 ($450). Mr. Schwind avoids Victorian and mission oak. The shop is located in an 1810 sea captain's residence built in the Federal style.

● **YORK**. *George Marshall Store.* Rachel B. Grieg. Lindsay Rd. 207-363-4974. Open May–Oct. and the Christmas season, daily 10–5. This shop represents the selected (by jury) works of about a hundred New England craftspeople working in most craft media. The shop also carries antique quilts. Among the craftspeople who exhibit here are Barbara Scarponi, silversmith; Richard Harkness, glassblower and Carol Summus, printmaker. The George Marshall

Store was built in 1867 and was a general store until 1955. It is located on the wharf at York River. It is a museum shop owned by Historic Landmarks of York County, Inc.

Georgeana Antiques. Norman and Julie Upham. Southside Rd. 207-363-3842. Open daily 9–5. Georgeana Antiques has a general line which excludes furniture, except for an occasional small piece, but includes memorabilia and collectibles. The shop line consists of those things found in area homes with prices based on the amount paid for the articles, not on book value.

Seacoast Crafts Fair. St. Christopher's-by-the-Sea. Rt. 1A (between York and York Village). 207-363-2397 or 207-363-4974 (Ms. R. B. Grieg). Open Wed.–Sat., last week in August. This annual event shows the work of fifty to sixty New England craftspeople whose admission to the fair is juried and whose work represents all crafts media.

NORTH COAST (Thomaston and north)

● **CALAIS**. *Dexter Shoe Factory Outlet* (see **Dexter**). Main St.

● **CAMDEN**. *Laurie V. Adams: Stoneware and Porcelain*. Upper Mountain St. (1½ mi. from town on left, Rt. 52). 207-236-8457. Open most weekdays 12–5; call to be certain. Laurie Adams sells her own original designs of functional pottery in subtle glazes. She makes porcelain and stoneware dinnerware, teapots, vases, and other functional items and a few sculptural pieces. She is a member of the Bay View Street Craft Cooperative, described below.

Bay View Street Craft Cooperative. A Maine Craft Co-op. 4 Bay View St. (next to the Brott Gallery). Open mid-June to Dec. Mon.–Sat. 10–5. This is a brand new craft cooperative featuring several craftspeople from Maine. Among them are Laurie Adams, potter; Jill Coyle Driscoll, potter; Jane Scholz, potter; Kathy Downs, jeweler; and Spruce and Deena, leatherworkers. The center features the works of these artists and probably will represent several more by the time of this printing. The Co-op exhibits and sells functional and decorative pottery, leather purses and clothing, jewelry (earrings from $7.50–$30 a pair) and Christmas Spirits in clay ($7.50 and up).

Rufus Foshee Antiques. Rufus and Joan Foshee. Rt. 1. (3½ mi. north on Rt. 1 from downtown). 207-236-2838. Open 10–5 daily all year. The Foshees are the most noted dealers in America for Spongeware, Spatterware, and White Patterned Ironstone. They have splendid collections of eighteenth- and early nineteenth-century English pottery and porcelain. The Foshees are avid gardeners so be sure to ask about their garden if you are interested.

The Gallery Shop of Camden. Nancy and Norman Holland. 82 Elm St. 207-236-4290. Open all year Mon.–Sat. 10–5. This shop carries a broad line of crafts including functional and decorative pottery, graphics, paintings, sculpture, imported folk art and craft, hand-made jewelry, blown glass, stained glass originals, dollhouse miniatures, ethnic clothing, silk screens, and hand-wrought iron. The shop is a nineteenth-century Victorian Home of fourteen rooms with the shop on the first floor. In the summer months the art work is displayed in an old hand-hewn barn.

Maine's Massachusetts House and Workshop. Bayview St. 207-236-8758. Open 10–5 daily April to Christmas. This is a branch of the main shop in Lincolnville (which see).

The Richards, Antiques. Barbara and Chad Richards. 93 Elm St. (Rt. 1). 207-236-2152. Open June–Oct. 9–5, except Wed. and Sun. Appointment advisable. The Richardses offer a general line of antiques with special emphasis on primitives and early lighting. They also carry some new lamp shades for the antique light fixtures.

Suffolk Gallery. 13 Elm St. 207-236-8868. Open year-round Mon.–Sat. 9:30–5:30, except two or three months in winter. The Suffolk gallery specializes in antiques and nineteenth-century paintings. Their selections include late eighteenth- and early nineteenth-century English furniture, English pottery and porcelain from 1750 to 1900, English and Continental paintings and drawings from 1840 to 1940, some glass, Oriental and Continental china, brass, jewelry, books, prints, etc. Recent offerings included an English chest-on-chest with bow front and mahogany veneer, c. 1835 ($1750), a Swansea bat printed Tea Service, c. 1815 ($350) a Doulton pitcher c. 1900 ($75), and a Joseph Farquharson dated and signed portrait, 1886 ($450). The shop also has a branch at 47 Bay View St. on the waterfront which is open from Memorial Day through Labor Day, 9:30–9:30.

● **ELLSWORTH**. *Cascade Woolen Fabric Mill Outlet* (see **Oakland**). Charles W. House and Sons—Cascade Woolen Mill. 125 High St. Open all year Mon.–Sat. 9:30–4:30.

Dexter Shoe Factory Outlet (see **Dexter**). Bar Harbor Rd. (Rt. 3).

Calista Sterling Antiques. Calista Sterling. Bayside Rd. (Rt. 230—alternate route to Bar Harbor). 207-667-8991. Open May–Sept. 9–6; by chance Oct.–Apr. Calista Sterling specializes in early period furniture, soft-paste china, and American primitives. She has two separate shops—formal and primitive. Recently she offered a Hepplewhite card table ($1500), strawberry soft-paste cups and saucers ($200 each) and a strawberry soft-paste sugar bowl ($260).

Strong Craft Gallery. Roslyn and Harris Strong. Bar Harbor Rd. 207-667-2595. Open in winter Mon.–Sat. 9–5; summer, daily 9–9. The Strongs are experienced and well-known craftspeople who select the finest work designed and made by more than 175 of the country's best craftspeople with a special emphasis on the northeast.

The Gallery features top quality crafts, including functional and decorative pottery, weaving, fiber arts, stone ware, jewelry, blown and stained glass and all varieties of metalwork. The Strongs also sell unusual yarns, small looms, and weaving accessories. The Gallery has a special sale January 10–30th.

● **LINCOLNVILLE**. *Maine's Massachusetts House.* Rt. 1. 207-789-5705. Open all year 9–6 daily (in winter, 9–5 Mon.–Sat. and closed Sun.). This shop is named after a historic building located diagonally across the street. Built in 1718, the little house was originally in that part of Maine that belonged to Massachusetts. This shop offers the selected crafts of over 100 New England craftspeople whose works include both functional and decorative pottery, hand-made jewelry, scrimshaw, wrought iron, traditional oils, water-colors and prints, woodcarving, mobiles, Chelsea clocks, and many other gift items. Craft demonstrations (pottery, woodcarving, printmaking, scrimshaw engraving, and painting) are scheduled for the summer and fall seasons at the gallery.

- **LUBEC**. *The Wharf Shop*. Water St. 207-733-4701. Open all year, daily 10–5. This shop is partially owned by the Lubec Crafts Council and offers functional and decorative pottery, silver and gold jewelry, Katrina tile panels, Jotul wood stoves, plants, and furniture.

- **MILLBRIDGE**. *Eastern Maine Crafts Co-op*. Main St. (on Rt. 1). Open June 15–Sept. 30 daily 10–5:30. The Co-op exhibits and sells the work of their designer craftspeople, who own and maintain the shop. Included are functional and decorative pottery, batik, jewelry, blacksmithing, metal sculpture, weaving, and brass bells. The prices here range from $2.50 for a stoneware mug to $150 for a large intricate piece of weaving or metalware. Some of the members are: Peter Weil, metal sculpture; Cherie Magnello, jewelry; Dawn Mann, batik; George Brace, blacksmithing; Sue Grasjean and Penelope Jerabek, weaving; and Charles Grosjean, Douglas Mann, and Dan Weaver, stoneware. The store, located in an old white frame house converted into an attractive gallery, is operated by members of the Eastern Maine Crafts Co-op who also act as salespeople.

- **NORTHEAST HARBOR**. *William D. Hocker, Inc*. Main St. 207-276-5131. Open Mon.–Sat. 9:30–5:30. Closed winters. William Hocker limits his stock to investment quality antiques and does not handle collectibles of any kind, nor does he carry glass, china, or Oriental rugs. His stock includes eighteenth-century furniture with the emphasis on Georgian mahogany and walnut, as well as seventeenth-, eighteenth-, and some early nineteenth-century copper and brass. Marine items include paintings and prints, early navigational instruments, telescopes, sixteenth- and seventeenth-century charts, journals, logs, and models. Recent offerings included a terrestrial/celestial telescope by Matthew Berge (c. 1800), a half model of a Maine coastal schooner, a sea chart by Wagenhaer (Dutch, 1588) and a Georgian triple-top games table in walnut (English, 1720).

• **ORLAND**. *H.O.M.E.* Rt. 1. 207-469-7961. The center is open 9–5 daily all year. H.O.M.E. is a multipurpose cooperative designed to provide assistance in a variety of ways to low-income families in the state of Maine. Among its programs are a Craft Cooperative, an educational facility for high-school dropouts (including general and crafts instruction), a crafts outlet, an outreach program, and Project Woodstove (providing free firewood for the elderly and for low-income families). Profits from the sale of crafts at their center provide funding for the other programs and the craft shop provides an incentive to individuals to learn a craft in as much as they are guaranteed an outlet for their newly learned skills. Crafts here include many products—pottery, weaving, toys, inlaid wooden pitchers, paintings, jams and jellies, and other products of cottage industries. The Annual H.O.M.E. Crafts Fair is held in mid-August at the center in Orland. Call or write for exact dates and times.

• **PORT CLYDE**. *Port Clyde General Store*. Bruce Waters. Main St. Open daily, all year, 8 A.M.–9 P.M. The Port Clyde General Store is a true general store; it dates from the turn of the century and still has the original fixtures. This is not a reconstruction for tourists, but the one and only store serving the Port Clyde area. The owners have added no gimmicks. They raise their own sheep and sell these native yarns for weavers and knitters. The store is also known for its fresh seafoods and local honey. This is a quiet place to browse while awaiting the ferry to Monhegan.

• **ROCKLAND**. *Van Baalen Pacific Corporation (Factory Outlet)*. 87–95 Camden St. 207-596-6646. Open Mon.–Fri. 9–4:30, Sat. 9–12. The factory outlet features discounts on men's bathrobes and swim wear and ladies lounge wear. The first quality items are discounted 25 percent and the seconds are 50–75 percent off retail prices.

• **ROCKPORT**. *Dexter Shoe Factory Outlet* (see **Dexter**). Rt. 1 at Glen Cove.

• **SEARSPORT**. *The Captain's House*. Mr. & Mrs. William W. Hoeseble. East Main St. (2½ mi. east of Searsport on Rts. 1

and 3). 207-548-6344. Open Apr.–Oct. daily 10–5. Other times by chance or appointment. The Captain's House carries period American furniture and accessories, Chinese export porcelain and a general line of antiques.

Morse and Applebee Antiques. Curtis and Sylvia Applebee Morse. Rt. 1 (½ mi. north of downtown). 207-548-6314. Open mid-Mar. to mid-Oct. 9–5. Other times by chance or appointment. The shop offers a wide variety of antique glassware, country things, and antique collectors' items of every type. There are fine collections of early American glassware, bottles, and nineteenth- and early twentieth-century Art Glass. The Applebee-Morses also carry unique small items of quality, country kitchen articles, and some country furniture with original finishes. They do *not* carry Depression glass and new collectible plates. The shop is located in a nineteenth-century sea captain's house (under restoration) overlooking the beautiful Penobscot Bay. This stretch of Rt. 1 in and around Searsport contains approximately twenty antique shops.

Rudder House. Mr. and Mrs. Roger B. Rudder. Rt. 1 (just out of Searsport center on left). 207-548-2570. Open all year by chance or appointment. The Rudders deal in antiques of the eighteenth and nineteenth centuries—primitives and fine furniture and accessories. They also specialize in tools and accessories. Their antiques are especially nice. The shop is in a large handsome sea captain's home restored by the Rudders. There is a wonderful big barn behind the house.

• **SOUTH THOMASTON**. *Keag River Pottery.* Tony and Nancy Oliver. Westbrook St. (just off Rt. 73). 207-594-7915. Open Memorial Day to Labor Day 9–6, Sun. 1–6. Closed Wed. Other times by appointment. Keag River is a small working pottery shop that makes stoneware on the premises. The potters are happy to make up special orders to the customers' own designs and styles. Seconds are available at reduced prices. The shop is located in a renovated barn attached to an 1806 Cape style house.

• **SPRUCE HEAD**. *Lobster Lane Book Shop.* Vivian York. Rt. 73. 207-594-7520. Open 12:30–5 daily mid-June–Sept. This small, old shop perched on the edge of the water in the lovely fishing village of Spruce Head Island is one of our favorite browsing spots in mid-coast Maine. The shop is crammed to the ceiling (literally) with old books and magazines, and is the perfect place to find a fun book or nostalgic magazine to dispell the gloom of a foggy or rainy day. In addition to the used books and magazines, there are some true out-of-print books that are of interest to collectors, and an occasional small antique.

• **STOCKTON SPRINGS**. *Victorian House and Book Barn*. Aimee B. MacEwen. East Main St. 207-567-3351. Open May–Oct. Mon.–Sat. 9–5; Nov.–April by appointment. Ms. MacEwen specializes in antiquarian, used, and out of print books from her large mid-nineteenth-century New England House.

• **THOMASTON**. *Maine State Prison Showroom*. Main St. (Rt. 1). 207-354-2535. Open daily in summer 9–5, winter 9–3. The Prison Showroom is a model in this country for the encouragement of the development of useful skills by prison inmates. All items for sale at the shop are made in the State Prison (next door) in the workshop. The front of the store is devoted to the sales of the factory production by inmates of forty-six different items of Colonial style maple furniture. Included are beds, dressers, chests, shelves, stools, lawn chairs, chairs, and more. The back of the shop is a gift shop that carries the craftwork of the inmates. These works are produced during the inmate's free time, and are not part of his factory responsibilities. Each craft item bears the maker's identification number and the proceeds of the sales of these crafts benefit that person directly. Typical crafts include anchor lamps, ship models, jewelry boxes, and games. Almost all are made of wood and wood products. Prices here are very low—a five-drawer Cape Cod chest is $145, and single maple bed frames are $75. The shop is run by the prison inmates who will be happy to answer any questions about the work for sale.

• **WEST BROOKLIN**. *Old Friends Barn*. Louisa Goodyear. 1 mi. from Sedgwick. 207-359-8949. Open 10–5 daily March–Nov., by appointment Dec.–Feb. Louisa Goodyear carries country antiques, specializing in old Maine furniture—restored and inexpensive. Recently the shop had a full-blown copper fighting-cock weathervane, including directionals and standard ($550), and a lovely old primitive pine jelly cupboard ($200). The shop is located in one section of an old barn, the other section of which is inhabited by sheep. After spring shearing, the natural yarn is sold at the shop.

• **WHITING**. *The Puffin' Pig*. Chuck and Marilyn Corthell. Rt. 1 (just south of turnoff to Roosevelt Park). 207-733-4670. Open Apr.–Dec. daily 9 A.M. to whenever. Jan.–Mar. open on request by ringing doorbell. The Puffin' Pig carries an assortment of gifts and crafts. The shop offers moccasins, shoes, firearms, and Indian crafts. There are deerskin purses and gloves, turquoise jewelry, about ninety styles of moccasins, and blown and cast glass. Sales are run in November and December.

INLAND

• **AUBURN**. *Glory Hole Antiques*. Linda DeStefano. 156 Turner St. 207-782-7593. Open 10–5 Mon.–Tues., Thurs.–Sat.; by appointment on Sun. The shop carries a varied line of general antiques with a special emphasis on Oriental antiques. Ms. DeStefano also offers silver, jewelry, furniture, books, art glass, primitives, paintings and prints.

• **AUGUSTA**. *Maine State Museum Gift Shop*. State House (in the State Capitol Complex). 207-289-2301. Open Mon., Wed., Fri. 9–4; Tues. and Thurs. 9–8; Sat.–Sun. 1–4. The Museum Gift Shop carries books on Maine, Maine crafts, and Maine gem stones. They also sell medals.

• **BANGOR**. *Dexter Shoe Factory Outlet* (see **Dexter**). 419 Main St.

Shadey Enterprises—Stained Glass Studio. Scott and Christy Kendrick. 44 Central St. (3rd floor) 207-947-6695 (evenings). Open Tues.–Sat. 10–4. The Kendricks specialize in custom-leaded and stained-glass lamps and windows. They make Tiffany-type lamps and original-design windows. They also carry stained glass and lead supplies.

• **BREWER**. *United Maine Craftsmen Annual Crafts Fair*. United Maine Craftsmen. Greater Bangor Area. Brewer Auditorium. Thanksgiving weekend. This is one of the biggest crafts fairs held in Maine. For exact dates and times call the United Maine Craftsmen (207-666-3447) or the local Chamber of Commerce.

● **BRIDGTON**. *The Cool Moose*. Peter Lowell. 102 Main St. 207-647-2446. Open in summer daily 10–5; in winter Fri. and Sat. 10–5. The Cool Moose claims to be the oldest year-round leather craft shop in the state. It carries all types of leather goods including a wide selection of belts with assorted special brass or bronze buckles, handbags, watchbands, clogs and sandals. Four workshops in and adjacent to the shop make it possible to do custom work in wood, leather, metals, and silk-screening.

● **CARIBOU**. *Caribou Sidewalk Arts and Crafts Festival*. Downtown streets. 207-492-5231. Early July. This is a one-day festival and features works in all media displayed by the artists and craftspeople at streetfront booths. Contact the Chamber of Commerce at the above number for details.

Dexter Shoe Factory Outlet (see **Dexter**). Caribou Skyway Plaza.

● **DENMARK**. *C. E. Guarino, Old Maps and Prints*. Berry Rd. (on Rt. 117 at the "Welcome to Denmark" sign). 207-452-2123. Mr. Guarino exhibits and sells antique maps and prints of seventeenth- to nineteenth-century Americana. He carries maps of American states and territories from the 1600s. Prints include American views, Currier and Ives, Kurz and Allison Civil War lithographs, and general Americana. He publishes eight catalogues yearly and carries *no* reproductions, limited editions, or facsimile pieces.

● **DEXTER**. *Dexter Shoe Factory Outlet*. Dexter Shoe Company. Railroad Ave. 207-924-7341 (headquarters). Open 9:30–9 P.M. during tourist months; hours vary at the many stores. The Dexter Shoe Outlets sell 85 percent Dexter Shoes; the rest of the shoes and leather belts are from other manufacturers including Converse. Dexter Shoes are sold throughout the United States in fine department stores, pro shops, sporting goods shops, and shoe stores. The Factory Outlets offer these same shoes at savings of up to 50 percent and more. Certain stores (there are many Dexter

Outlets throughout Maine and New Hampshire) sell factory-damaged shoes for an even greater savings. Some of the Outlets are located at the factories and others are in Dexter log cabins in Maine and New Hampshire.

- **DOUGLAS HILL.** *Glass Basket Antiques.* Miss Dorothy-Lee Jones. off Rt. 107. 207-787-3527. Open June–Sept. Mon.–Sat. 10:30–5. This shop has an unusually large, excellent collection of early glass, including both Eastern and Western American blown, pressed, lacy and pattern glass, art glass, art nouveau and art deco. In addition it carries English, French, and general continental glass types as well as ceramics (mostly nineteenth-century English). Recent offerings included a Thomas Caines, South Boston Glass decanter and plate, c. 1820 ($450 for the set); a lacy Sandwich 10 in. plate ($1000); and a Burmere 10 in. plate ($350). Miss Jones has a special exhibition room of museum quality pieces which are not for sale; parts of her collection can be found in five major museums.

- **DRESDEN.** *Yankee Peddler Day.* Pownalborough Court House. Rt. 128 between Rts. 27 and 197. 207-882-6817. The Lincoln County Cultural and Historical Association sponsors the Yankee Peddler Day in early August.

- **FRYEBURG.** *Northland Shoe Factory Outlet.* 58 Main St. (Rt. 302, 1 mi. from the New Hampshire line). 207-935-2540. Open 9–5 seven days a week in summer. The Shoe Outlet features men's and women's shoes and boots at discount prices. The shop carries first quality at reduced rates and excellent discounts on seconds and cancellations.

- **GORHAM.** *Hanson's Carriage House.* Jean and Arn Hanson. Main St. 207-839-6092. Open all year, daily 9–5 and by appointment. The Hansons offer 90 percent antiques and 10 percent collectibles (Shaker memorabilia). They are most comfortable with early American country antiques and carry country furniture, textiles, and Shaker and other primitives. All their antiques are hand-rubbed in keeping with the original paint or finish of the piece. The shop is located in their lovely old white clapboard carriage house with a barn next door.

- **GUILFORD.** *Guilford Mill Store.* Guilford Industries, Inc.

Oak St. 207-876-3331. Open year-round Mon.–Sat. 8:30–5, Sun. 12–5. The Mill Store is located right at the mill and features fabrics for all seasons—upholstery, drapery, screen fabric and patterns, notions, and camp blankets. The store has several sales throughout the year and two big sales, one in August and the other in January.

 • **HALLOWELL**. Hallowell is a suburb of Augusta and deserves special mention because it has become the antiques capital of the state, with more than twenty antiques shops in the small historic downtown area. Hallowell was recently named a National Historic District and the area is known for its beautiful early sea captain's homes. Water Street, in particular, is the site of many of the shops. When in any shop, ask for a free pamphlet that will direct you to any of the other shops in the village.

Schneider's Antiques. Marianne Schneider. 130 Water St. 207-622-0002. Open Apr. 1–Dec. Mon.–Fri. 10–5; by chance Sat. and Sun. Jan.–March. Marianne Schneider specializes in mocha, tools, old toys, primitives, and the unusual. She also carries a general line of antiques but *no* glass. Recently there was a Carey's Celestial Globe, 1800 ($350), a two-side lollipop butter stamp ($375), and a miniature Windsor settee, original ($385). The shop is located in a four-story brick building c. 1800—once the tallest building north of Boston.

Sherrymike Pottery and Gallery. Adele Nichols. 207-622-1906. Open Mon.–Sat. 10–5. This shop carries the pottery of its owner as well as a broad line of other crafts which include functional and decorative pottery, weaving, spinning, fiber arts, graphics, painting, stoneware, jewelry, leather, stained glass, metalwork, blown glass, and sculpture. Among the many craftspeople who exhibit at the store are Stell and Shevis, Kate and Fred Pearce, Steve and Judy Brown, Jack Hemingway, Cathy Downs, and Ron Coles.

 • **HARMONY**. *Bartlettyarns, Inc.* South Rd. (Rt. 150 out of Skowhegan, about 20 mi.). 207-683-2251. Open Mon.–Fri. 8:30–4. Bartlettyarns features woolen yarns made right at the factory here. The shop also carries knitting machines and accessories, looms and weaving accessories, pattern books, and natural dyes. The store prices are the same as mail order prices, usually ⅔ to ¾ of the prices at retail outlets. The historic mill was started in 1821, and the present equipment is nineteenth-century. It is the only mill in the United States that still uses the old-fashioned "mule" for spinning woolen yarn.

• **HOULTON**. *Dexter Shoe Factory Outlet* (see **Dexter**). Houlton Skyway Plaza.

• **LEWISTON**. *Annual Christmas Crafts Fair*. Lewiston Armory. 207-782-6412. Early Dec. This fair, now in its eleventh year, is sponsored by the Central Maine Arts and Crafts Guild of Auburn and displays the work of its members.

Dexter Shoe Factory Outlet (see **Dexter**). 1035 Lisbon St. Bonneau Plaza.

A. J. Flies. A. J. Rector. Old Lisbon Rd. 207-782-5051. Open evenings by appointment. Mr. Rector makes a wide variety of flies for fishing in Maine waters and elsewhere for trout, salmon, and bass as well as salt water flies for casting and trolling. Mr. Rector was the originator of the "A. J. Locust" trout fly. In addition to single flies and combination packages, he sells feathered jewelry for men and women and a large assortment of fly-tying materials and equipment.

• **LINCOLN**. *Dexter Shoe Factory Outlet* (see **Dexter**). 87 Lee St.

• **LITCHFIELD**. *The Country House*. Helen B. and Allan B. Smith. Upper Pond Rd. 207-737-2870. Open by appointment only. The Smiths have written and published five books on salt dips. They are known and visited by collectors of salts from all over the country. The Country House specializes, exclusively, in individual open salt dips. The shop (not an open shop) is located in the Smiths' home, a lovely early nineteenth-century farmhouse.

• **LOVELL**. *Lovell Pewter*. Ken and Joan Kantro. Old Waterford Rd. 207-925-2032. Open May–Nov. 10–5 daily except Mon., other times by appointment. This shop is limited to the production of hand-cast, spun, and wrought pewter all of which are made in the workshop-showroom. Visitors may watch the crafting process.

• **MADAWASKA**. *Acadian Crafts Association, Inc.* Crafts Co-operative—Wholesale Shipping Business. 29 St. Catherine St. (just off Rt. 1). 207-728-3295. Call for hours. Acadian Crafts is a locally initiated, self-help co-operative, owned and operated by its members. The Acadian Crafts began in 1970 as a means of supplementing family incomes by carrying on the traditions of the women in the northernmost part of Aroostook County—that of crocheting baby clothes—a tradition dating back to the French Acadians in 1755. The co-op specializes in the crocheting and knitting of infants' clothing for catalog sales. For free catalog and price list contact the Co-operative.

Dexter Shoe Factory Outlet (see **Dexter**). Valley Shopping Plaza.

● **MILO**. *Basketville*. Main St. (from Rts. 16 and 6, off I-95). Open daily all year (see **Putney, VT**).

Dexter Shoe Factory Outlet (see **Dexter**). Main St.

● **NEW PORTLAND**. *Nowetah's American Indian Craft and Gift Shop*. Mrs. Nowetah Timmerman. Rt. 27. 207-628-4981. Open all year, seven days a week, 10–4. Mrs. Nowetah Timmerman is a Susquehanna-Cherokee Indian who operates her craft shop, which specializes in 100 percent wool handwoven rugs, blankets, and table mats. A demonstration loom is on display to show how the work is done on home-made primitive looms (not harness looms). Also made at the shop is American Indian beadwork. The shop also produces leather vests, pocketbooks, fur handbags, hand-blown glass jewelry and animals, shell animals, quilts, and other small items. Nowetah is most insistent that shoppers realize that all items are made by native Americans with no imported imitation Indian goods. The shop is contained in a traditional log building which the Timmermans built themselves. In addition to the shop items there is a small museum display of old Indian museum pieces depicting past American Indian life. The shop is not visible from the road, but there is a sign with an Indian head at the entrance to its driveway.

● **NEWFIELD**. *Christmas Etcetera*. Willowbrook at Newfield. Off Rt. 11. 207-793-2784. Open May 15–Dec. 23 daily 11–5. Closed Thanksgiving. Christmas Etcetera is said to be the second largest gift shop in Maine. Although the emphasis in this book is on crafts, antiques, and factory outlets, this shop with its very large selection of gifts, cards, candles, lamps, stocking stuffers, and wooden items is included because of its location in Newfield, one of New England's most important historical restorations. This collection of restored barns, shops, and houses is open from May 15 to September 30 and is more fully described in *The Country New England Sightseeing and Historical Guide*.

• **NORTH BERWICK**. *Hilton's Antiques*. Gordon and Charlotte Hilton. Oak Woods Rd. (follow signs off Rt. 4 between Sanford and North Berwick). 207-676-5570. Open year-round 9–5. The Hiltons carry country antiques. They specialize in country furniture, primitives, and old tools. The shop is located in a 1765 farmhouse.

Donald and Lois Tucker Antiques. Elm St. 207-676-4429. Open year-round by chance or appointment. This shop is limited to china and a small selection of pre-1830 pieces. China specialties include historical Staffordshire, creamware, pearlware, mocha, flow blue ironstone, spatterware, and Liverpool. Recent offerings included a 16-inch Cape Coast Castle historical blue platter ($575), a pillar and scroll shelf clock, Eli and Samuel Terry, with full label ($2000), and a Scinde flow blue washbowl and pitcher ($425). The Tuckers avoid Victorian items. Their shop is located in a c. 1800 Federal house with fanlight and palladian window.

• **NORTH WINDHAM**. *Dexter Shoe Factory Outlet* (see **Dexter**). North Windham Shopping Center.

• **OAKLAND**. *The Mill Store*. Cascade Woolen Mill Factory Outlet. Fairfield St. (take I-95N, to Oakland-Waterville exit, west on Rt. 137). 207-465-2511. Open all year Mon.–Sat. 8:30–4:30. The store carries a large stock of wool and wool blends, all made at the mill starting from raw stock. It also sells 100 percent washable polyesters. There is a huge selection of wool blankets (60" × 84") at discount prices. All yard goods are sold at 50–60 percent of normal retail price. Remnants and seconds are sold by the pound, as are discontinued fabrics and styles. The Cascade Mill building dates back to 1882 when it was run by water power.

• **PITTSTON**. *Phipps of Pittston*. Maggie Phipps. Benedict Arnold Rd. 207-582-3555. Open 10–5 spring–fall. Closed Sun. Maggie Phipps specializes in furniture, antique pottery and decorator items including refinished pine and maple (especially tables, chests, cupboards, and chairs), quilts, copper, brass and sponge-ware, ironstone, and some glass and china. Recent offerings included a set of four pine plank-seat chairs with thumb backs ($195), and a pine and maple two-piece cupboard ($795). Her shop avoids overnight collectibles.

• **PRESQUE ISLE**. *Dexter Shoe Factory Outlet* (see **Dexter**). 328 Main St.

• **RICHMOND**. *The Loft*. Kay Pierce. 9 Gardiner St. (three blocks off Main St.). 207-737-2056. Open all year by chance or appointment. The Loft specializes in nineteenth-century clothing, quilts, jewelry, and decorative items. Kay Pierce also carries china and pressed glass and a small amount of furniture (pie safe, china cupboard, and some tables). She specifically avoids depression glass and carnival glass. Recently Kay had c. 1840 ladies bonnets ($22–$35) and a child's beaver hat ($35), there was a lovely set of six-ivory carved teaspoons ($150), and a large sampler ($175). The Loft is located in the carriage loft of a huge Victorian house built by Joseph Spaulding in 1869. The village is full of wonderful old sea captain's homes.

• **SABATTUS**. *Grab Bag Antiques*. Alan Grab. 39 Main St. (exit 13 off Maine Tpk. to Rt. 126, about 5 mi. out). 207-375-4711. Open all year, seven days a week 9 A.M. to dusk. Alan Grab specializes in refinished oak furniture. He carries an extensive line of round oak tables, oak ice boxes, hall trees, and sets of pressed back chairs.

• **SANFORD**. *Dexter Shoe Factory Outlet* (see **Dexter**). Midtown Shopping Center.

• **SKOWHEGAN**. *Brick Farm Shop*. James P. Hastings. West Ridge Rd. 207-474-3949. Open Apr. 1–Dec. 24 daily 10–5. The Brick Farm Shop handles a wide range of crafts in almost all media. Each fall from October 1 through Christmas, the shop sponsors a weekly craft demonstration on Sunday afternoons. The shop is in a converted horse barn which was built in 1850.

Dexter Shoe Factory Outlet (see **Dexter**). West Front St. Rt. 2.

• **THORNDIKE**. *Bryant Steel Works*. Joseph and Beatrice Bryant. Off Rt. 139 and 137. 207-568-3663. Open all year Mon.–

Sat. 7–6. The Steel Works is an Antique Stove Museum, where 150–200 stoves on a show floor are offered for sale. The Bryants carry antique stoves, kitchen cook stoves, box heaters and fireplaces. They recently had a parlor heater with magnificent brass accessories for $600, and there are kitchen stoves for about $950.

• **UNION**. *Abbott-Wheat Country Studio.* Veronica Gigante Abbott. 207-785-4656. Open 9–5 by chance and by appointment. Ms. Abbot describes herself as an artist-designer, as contrasted to a production craftsperson. Her studio carries a diversified line of one-of-a-kind works including wall hangings in applique and batik, paintings, some wearable art and accessories, character dolls for collectors, surface stitchery panels, leaded glass ornaments and figures, sailing ships created to scale, and designer crochet hats. Ms. Abbott has exhibited her work at about twenty-five galleries around the country including the National Academy Galleries, New York; the Hecksher Museum, New York; The Huntington Art League, New York; Phoenix Art Museum, Phoenix; Colorado Springs Art Center, Colorado; Farnsworth Museum, Rockland, Maine; and Springfield Art Museum, Missouri.

• **WATERVILLE**. *Dexter Shoe Factory Outlet* (see **Dexter**). J.F.K. Plaza.

Hathaway Shirts Factory Outlet. C. F. Hathaway Co. 10 Water St. 207-873-4241. Open regular business hours including weekends. The Factory Outlet offers men's and women's Hathaway shirts at greatly reduced prices. They have men's dress shirts for $11; ladies shirts, $12; golf shirts, $10; Dior shirts, $13; Dior ties, $6; and sportsshirts, $10–$20.

Silver St. Gallery. 8 Silver St. 207-873-2234. Open Tues.–Sat. 11–5. This shop is a cooperative effort of twelve Maine craftspeople, and carries hand-made items only. These include functional and decorative pottery, weaving, graphics, stoneware, jewelry, leather, wooden toys, quilts, and wooden bowls and dishes. Some examples of craftwork available at the store include a hand-forged silver necklace ($30), a stoneware bowl ($10) and a leather handbag ($45).

• **WELLINGTON**. *The Schoolhouse.* Gretchen and Michael Moore. Harmony Rd. (call for directions). 207-683-2814. Open by chance or appointment. The Moores sell their own original designs of wooden, handpainted jigsaw puzzles, dolls, and block sets which are used as teaching aids. The Schoolhouse is their workshop, but visitors are welcome to see the crafts sold here. A moose puzzle sells for $18, a reversible puzzle "Winter–Summer" is $26, and pigtailed girl doll is $15.

● **WEST LEBANON**. *The Little Horse Antique Shop.* Bill and Thelma Howell. Milton Rd. 207-658-4543. Open by chance or by appointment. This shop is located only ½ mile from Milton, N.H., and carries a general line of antiques with the emphasis on old lamps and lighting devices.

● **WILTON**. *Dexter Shoe Factory Outlet* (see **Dexter**). Jct. Rts. 2 and 4.

Index